—Diseases and People—

DEPRESSION

Alvin and Virginia Silverstein
and Laura Silverstein Nunn

Enslow Publishers, Inc.

44 Fadem Road	PO Box 38
Box 699	Aldershot
Springfield, NJ 07081	Hants GU12 6BP
USA	UK

Library of Congress Cataloging-in-Publication Data

Silverstein, Alvin.
    Depression / Alvin and Virginia Silverstein and Laura Silverstein
Nunn.
        p. cm. — (Diseases and people)
    Includes bibliographical references and index.
    Summary: Discusses the causes, symptoms, and treatments of
depression, examining the different types of depression and their
effects on the individual and on society.
    ISBN 0-89490-713-1
    1. Depression, Mental—Juvenile literature. [1. Depression,
Mental.] I. Silverstein, Virginia B. II. Nunn, Laura Silverstein.
III. Title. IV. Series.
RC537.S536 1997
616.85'27—DC21

                                                97-1789
                                                CIP
                                                AC

Printed in the United States of America

10 9 8 7 6 5 4 3

Illustration Credits: The Bettmann Archive, pp. 27, 64, 79; Corbis-Bettmann,
p. 62; Courtesy of the National Library of Medicine, pp. 10, 15, 17, 19, 22, 24, 33,
41, 44, 76, 88, 93; Reprinted with special permission of King Features Syndicate,
p. 98; UPI/Bettmann, pp. 29, 66, 69; UPI/Corbis-Bettmann, p. 50.

Cover Illustration: © 1996 John-Marshall Mantel/Tom Keller & Associates

Contents

Acknowledgments

The authors would like to thank J. Michael Murphy, Ed.D, assistant professor of psychology, Harvard Medical School and licenced psychologist, Massachusetts General Hospital, for his careful reading of the manuscript and many helpful comments. Also, many thanks to Isabel Davidoff and Denise Juliano-Bult at the Depression Awareness, Recognition, and Treatment Program, National Institute of Mental Health for their suggestions and the information they provided.

DEPRESSION

What is it? A chronic mood disorder characterized by persistent feelings of sadness, hopelessness, and irritability. The most severe form is referred to as major depression; a milder form that tends to continue for long periods is dysthymia; cyclic periods of depression alternating with exaggerated "highs" make up manic-depressive illness, also called bipolar disorder. Recurrent episodes of depression, influenced by the seasons of the year, are termed seasonal affective disorder (SAD).

Who gets it? People of all ages, all races, and both sexes. Women outnumber men in cases of clinical depression (those severe enough to require treatment), but the difference may be due to the greater reluctance of men to seek help.

How do you get it? Researchers believe that people inherit a tendency toward depression; actual episodes may be triggered by stressful life events such as the loss of a loved one.

What are the symptoms? Feelings of sadness, helplessness, hopelessness, and irritability; change of appetite; change in sleeping patterns; loss of interest and pleasure; fatigue; feelings of worthlessness and guilt; difficulty in concentrating; recurring thoughts of death or suicide; disturbed thought patterns; and physical symptoms including headache, backache, and stomachache. (A person may not experience all of these symptoms.) The manic phase of bipolar disorder may be characterized by strong feelings of happiness and confidence, fast talking, great energy and reduced need for sleep, irrational thought patterns and unrealistic ideas and plans, obnoxious behavior, and sometimes increased creativity.

How is it treated? With antidepressant drugs (e.g., Prozac), with psychotherapy, and with electroconvulsive therapy (ECT or shock therapy); bipolar depression is treated with salts of the metal lithium.

How can it be prevented? Some episodes of depression may be prevented by learning techniques to reduce and handle life's stresses. Continuous lithium therapy can prevent recurrences of bipolar cycles.

1

Feeling Blue

braham Lincoln is considered one of the greatest leaders in American history, still admired for his combination of honesty, common sense, and humor. Every day, he had to make important decisions as a part of his duties as the president of the United States. But Lincoln had a dark side. He was actually a very moody person who suffered from both mild and severe bouts of depression.[1] Lincoln's depression seemed to worsen when his good friend Ann Rutledge died in 1835. A few years later, Abraham Lincoln began a stormy relationship with his new love, Mary Todd. In January of 1841, Lincoln broke off their engagement and fell deeper into depression. At one point his friends became so worried about Lincoln's mental state that they watched over him and did not allow him to have any knives or other dangerous objects. In a letter to Mary Todd, Lincoln revealed the severity of his depression: "I am now the most miserable man living. If what I feel were equally distributed to the whole human family, there would not be one cheerful face on earth. Whether I shall ever be better, I cannot tell; I awfully forebode I shall not."[2] Mary Todd's family thought he was insane. Abraham Lincoln and Mary Todd finally married in 1842. But even on his wedding day, Lincoln remained depressed with suicidal thoughts and feelings of worthlessness.[3]

It seems hard to believe that a man like Lincoln, who was so level-headed and held such an important job, could be tormented by depression. Yet this is a chronic disease that can affect anyone, anywhere, and at any time. Abraham Lincoln was only one of many famous people who was plagued by depression over thousands of years of history.

Everyone gets "the blues" from time to time, but clinical depression is a more serious condition. Simply feeling depressed is only part of the disease. People who are clinically depressed have a variety of symptoms, such as feeling "down in the dumps," sleep disturbances, eating disorders, and lack of energy. These symptoms become so overwhelming that the person may be unable to function normally in everyday activities.

Depression comes in different forms. Major depression can range from mild to severe. Dysthymia is a milder form of depression that can last for years. Seasonal affective disorder (SAD) is a form of depression that occurs at the same time each year, according to the change of seasons. In manic-depressive illness the person's mood goes through cycles, alternating between exaggerated feelings of happiness and confidence and feelings of deep misery. Each type of depression has similar symptoms, with slight variations. People experience depressive illnesses differently—some have mild symptoms, while others suffer severe symptoms.

Scientists do not know what really causes clinical depression. They believe that there may not be a single cause, but possibly a combination of factors. Environmental factors (for example, the loss of a job or loved one), psychological factors (negative thinking, low self-esteem), genetic factors (is a gene to blame?), and biochemical factors (chemical imbalance in the brain) may all contribute to depression.

Scientists believe that for many people with depression, something has gone wrong in the biochemical processes in the brain. The brain releases special chemicals, such as serotonin, that regulate a person's mood. In depressed patients, somehow the chemicals in the brain become imbalanced, with either too much or not enough of the key hormones. As a result, the person's mood starts to go to extremes.

There are two major types of treatment for depression: drug treatment and psychotherapy. Drug treatment includes a wide variety of medications, called antidepressants. This type of treatment is usually most effective for patients who have a chemical imbalance in the brain. The purpose of antidepressants is to bring the chemicals in the brain back to a normal level. One of the most popular and controversial antidepressants is Prozac. However, drugs work differently for

This is an illustration of depression, or "melancholia," from a medical textbook published in 1892.

different people. What works like magic for one person can be dangerous to another.

Psychotherapy, or "talk therapy," involves a patient talking with a therapist to understand and resolve conflicts. It is generally helpful in cases of mild to moderate depression. The various types of psychotherapy include behavioral therapy, cognitive therapy, family therapy, group therapy, interpersonal therapy, psychoanalytic therapy, and psychodynamic therapy. Many mental health specialists agree that the most effective treatment is a combination of both drug and psychological treatment.

Depression has had a profound effect on society. It can make people unable to function at school and work. Some even have to be hospitalized. Depression has cost society billions of dollars from lost work and medical expenses.

Depression can be fatal: Severe depression may lead to suicide. Unfortunately, the rate of depression is increasing, and so is the rate of suicide, especially among teenagers. People with suicidal tendencies need immediate attention. Hospitalization may be necessary to save a person's life. Unfortunately, society puts a stigma on people who suffer from emotional problems. Moreover, men often view depression as a sign of weakness. These attitudes can be dangerous to the people who are clinically depressed and refuse to get professional help. Some turn to alcohol and drugs rather than risking ridicule from others. This only adds more problems to an already difficult situation.

Many scientists believe that one or more genes are responsible for the occurrence of depression in some people. They continue to do research on this possibility. However, they have yet to find a "guilty gene." Some scientists are convinced that they will find the genes responsible for depression, and this knowledge will allow them to develop better methods for diagnosis, devise more effective treatments, and eventually find a way to prevent depression.

2

Depression in History

Written descriptions of depression date back to biblical times. Saul, who became the first king of Israel, suffered from severe mood swings. Often he sank into such black moods that people said an evil spirit was possessing him. Saul's servants suggested that having someone play the harp might soothe the king and help him to get through the bad nights. They recommended a young shepherd named David, who became a valued member of the royal household. Later David killed Goliath, the giant champion of Israel's enemies. Saul grew jealous of David's instant popularity, and his black moods returned. He had many violent outbursts and plotted to kill David. Saul's hostility and rage eventually led to a war in which he and his sons were killed in battle. David then became the king of Israel.[1]

Melancholia

In 400 B.C., Hippocrates, the Greek physician considered to be the father of medicine, described depression and called it *melancholia* (from Greek words meaning "black bile"). This ancient word was used to distinguish normal sad feelings from the negative feelings related to clinical depression.[2] The Greek philosopher Democritus also wrote about melancholia around 400 B.C. and studied its causes and treatments. The ancient Greeks and the Roman philosophers and physicians who followed them believed that the body is composed of four main substances, or "humors": phlegm, blood, choler, and black bile. The proportions of these humors determined a person's basic personality—phlegmatic (even-tempered, unemotional), sanguine (cheerful), choleric (hot-tempered), and melancholic.[3]

The fifteenth and sixteenth centuries were turbulent times in Europe, filled with conflict and confusion. Returning crusaders had brought back a ferment of new ideas and inventions, and explorers were discovering new lands. The invention of the printing press meant that knowledge could spread widely rather than being restricted to small groups of monks and scholars. Artists and philosophers were reexamining the classics and absorbing the new discoveries, as the Middle Ages gave way to the Renaissance. Revolutionary religious leaders such as Martin Luther challenged the authority of the Catholic Church, while some philosophers placed a new emphasis on human concerns. Yet, many of the old traditions and superstitions remained strong, and the constant threat of

Two great ancient physicians, Hippocrates (on the right) and Galen (on the left), were familiar with various forms of depression.

death shadowed the daily life of the people as deadly plagues continued to sweep periodically through the population.

Many of the artistic works of the time reflected the new mood of conflict and inner searching. One of the most famous is an engraving by the German artist Albrecht Dürer, entitled *Melancholia I.* In this masterpiece, completed in 1514, a woman sits in a courtyard filled with scattered tools, staring blankly into space. The picture is filled with symbols of doom that reinforce the feeling of depression, such as a starving dog, a sad-looking cupid, and a bat whose spread wings form a banner with the title of the work.[4] "You can see the essence of melancholia for the first time: the way in which the individual is caught in a trance, in a preoccupation with themselves, with all the tools of effort around the individual lying idle," comments Dr. Peter C. Whybrow, professor of psychiatry at the University of Pennsylvania. "It's a very ancient disturbance, this particular illness, and it has been known to man since we started to write about our own experience."[5]

A century after Dürer, Robert Burton, an English scholar and clergyman, wrote a book on depression, *The Anatomy of Melancholy.* In it he expanded on the theories of Democritus, updated to the view of Burton's own time. In the preface, Burton defended his writing on a medical subject with the argument that melancholy is both a spiritual and a bodily illness. The four parts of the book discuss the causes and symptoms of melancholy, its cure (Burton emphasized the importance of living in good air), love melancholy, and religious melancholy. The book, published in 1621, was a

German artist Albrecht Dürer completed his symbolic picture of melancholy in 1514.

best-seller in its time and went through five revised editions in the thirty years that followed.[6]

Seasonal Affective Disorder

Hippocrates identified a type of depression that was related to the change of seasons, now called seasonal affective disorder (SAD).[7] He noticed that people would become sad during the wintertime when there was less sunlight because of the shortened days. However, seasonal affective disorder has actually been rediscovered several times in history. In the 1800s it was recorded that psychiatrist Jean Etienne Esquirol was the first to identify this seasonal disorder.[8] However, it was not until the mid-1980s that SAD was officially recognized as a mood disorder. Dr. Norman E. Rosenthal, a researcher with the National Institutes of Health, was the first to use the term SAD and discovered a link between a change in behavior patterns and the onset of winter. In 1987 the American Psychiatric Association accepted seasonal affective disorder as a true mental disorder.[9]

Treatment for SAD patients actually dates back to the second century A.D., when Greek and Roman doctors realized that lack of sunlight was the key to treatment and proceeded to treat patients by directing sunlight toward their eyes. Until well into the 1900s, doctors advised their SAD patients to travel south for the winter. Before World War II, most hospitals were built with a solarium, or sunroom. European doctors treated SAD patients with a "light bath," called heliotherapy. It was named after Helios, the Greek god of the sun.

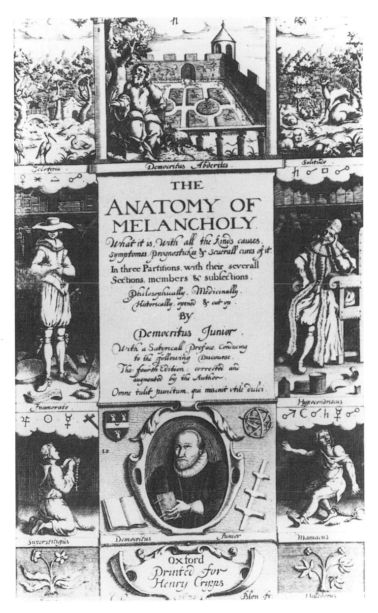

This is the title page from *The Anatomy of Melancholy* by
Robert Burton, first published in 1621.

Heliotherapy made a comeback in 1984 when Norman E. Rosenthal published his first paper on SAD and the use of light therapy to treat SAD.[10]

Manic-Depressive Disorder

In the early 1900s, German psychiatrist Emil Kraepelin described another form of depression, called manic depression. He studied several hundred patients with this condition, which is characterized by periods of mood swings from wild euphoria to deep despair. Although there were two parts to this illness, Kraepelin considered this a "single disease process" and tried to determine its nature and causes. He carefully examined the brains of his patients who had died, but he was unable to find any major differences from normal brains. He was also unable to come up with an effective treatment for the disorder. Other psychiatrists saw these negative results as evidence that manic-depressive illness was a disease of the mind, not the body, and felt that psychoanalysis would be an appropriate treatment. But it was soon realized that psychoanalysis did not work on severely depressed or manic patients.[11]

Early Treatment Was Barbaric

It was not until about fifty years ago that researchers were able to find truly effective treatments for patients with emotional disorders. Throughout history, people with a mental illness were often disregarded or treated rather brutally. In the early

1900s a lack of effective treatment caused doctors to keep severely mentally ill patients locked up in institutions without any hope of recovery.[12] In ancient Phoenicia the mentally ill were boarded on ships, known as the "ships of fools," and sailed out to sea to find another place that would care for them. In the Middle Ages, exorcists were used to remove the "demons" from the bodies of those who acted strangely. In the eighteenth century, "shock" treatments were administered to patients by twirling them on stools until their ears bled and by dropping them through trap doors into icy lakes.[13] Other eighteenth-century doctors wrapped electric eels around their patients' heads as a crude form of electric shock therapy.[14]

Shock Therapy

Shock therapy has changed a lot since the early days. The public knew very little about *electroconvulsive therapy*, or shock therapy, until it was dramatized in Mary Jane Ward's 1948 novel, *The Snake Pit*. The heroine, Virginia Cunningham, is hospitalized after she suffers a nervous breakdown. She finds herself being strapped down to an operating table, unable to move her arms. She feels a cold, smelly paste put on each of her temples and metal clamps attached over the paste. The attendant takes hold of her ankles. As the nurse forces a gag into her mouth, Virginia wonders what she could have done to deserve such torture. This form of treatment may sound horrifying, but it was actually an accurate account of what happened during shock therapy. What seemed like cruel punishment to Virginia was intended to protect her from the

This illustration of a "maniaque" is from a book on mental illness by Jean Etienne Esquirol, published in 1838.

intensity of the treatment. The gag in her mouth was there to keep her teeth from clenching. The hand and foot restraints were there to prevent bone fractures. However, the treatment caused Virginia to go through periods of memory loss. Once *The Snake Pit* was made into a movie, shock therapy became a hot topic of conversation. This resulted in a public controversy over the value and safety of shock therapy.[15]

Since then, however, electroconvulsive therapy has greatly improved, and its barbaric accompaniments are no longer used. Doctors will usually administer shock therapy only to severely depressed patients. It is a useful option when other methods have failed.

Antidepressants Are Discovered

Salts of the metal lithium have long been used as a medical treatment. Almost two thousand years ago, the physician Soranus of Ephesus treated depression and manic-depressive illness with mineral water, which most likely contained lithium.[16] About eighteen hundred years ago, the Greek physician Galen treated mania by having his patients bathe in alkaline springs and by having them drink from the waters. Lithium was probably present in the springs.[17]

In the nineteenth and twentieth centuries, mineral baths and spas became very popular in Europe and America because of their healing powers. People who were suffering from nervous breakdowns would be sent there for mineral-water treatment.[18]

Soranus of Ephesus treated manic depression with mineral waters nearly two thousand years ago.

Until 1949, however, no one knew what active ingredient in the mineral waters was responsible for their beneficial effects. An Australian psychiatrist, John Cade, discovered lithium's mood-altering properties by accident. Cade analyzed the urine of his manic patients, hoping to find a toxin that was responsible for triggering the abnormal behavior. He expected that this toxin would be similar to uric acid, a normal chemical in urine that is produced when the body processes proteins. Cade needed a form of uric acid that dissolved easily in water, and he picked lithium urate. When he tested the lithium urate on guinea pigs, he noticed that they became very sluggish. Cade then tried this chemical on his manic patients, and the results were astonishing. Eighty percent of his patients responded positively to the treatment. However, it was not until the 1970s that lithium was finally given FDA approval for the treatment of manic-depressive illness.[19] Lithium treatments are usually started during the manic phase. After the patient's mood has been normalized, the treatment is continued on a maintenance basis to prevent the manic-depression cycles from beginning again.[20]

In the 1950s researchers found that a new antituberculosis drug, called iproniazid, produced significant mood elevation in some patients. This finding was so striking that researchers started to investigate the mood-altering properties of the drug. They were excited about this new development and started to work on other antidepressant drugs. This led to a wide selection of antidepressant drugs that are now available to psychiatrists.[21]

3

What Is Depression?

Mike Wallace, CBS News reporter and correspondent for the show *60 Minutes,* has always called himself "pessimistic by nature."[1] However, it was not until 1984, when General William Westmoreland filed a libel suit against Wallace and his employer concerning a story Wallace did about Vietnam, that he realized what he was feeling was more serious than simply the blues. Wallace had to sit in a courtroom for five months, listening to the plaintiff's side of the story. Newspaper reports of the trial called Wallace a cheat and a liar. Wallace would walk into a restaurant and feel like everyone was pointing at him and looking at him with accusing eyes. After a while, he started to feel as though he really was the terrible person people said he was.

Wallace's feelings of hopelessness continued to grow. He could no longer sleep, he lost weight, and he felt pains in his

Mike Wallace, CBS News correspondent and co-editor of *60 Minutes,* suffered from depression.

arms and legs. Wallace once described his depression as feeling "lower than a snake's belly."[2] His mind was no longer his own. He was losing his memory and his concentration. If he read an article in the newspaper, he was unable to remember what it was about two minutes later. He was also having trouble conducting interviews and could not remember what questions he was supposed to ask.

Mike Wallace decided to go on vacation to St. Martin. Maybe he just needed a break, and this dreadful feeling would be gone by the time he got back home. The change of scene, however, failed to relieve his depression. He could not enjoy any of the activities he used to. He loved to play tennis, but he could not even muster up any enthusiasm to watch tennis pro Ivan Lendl, who happened to be practicing there. Instead, Wallace started to have thoughts about suicide.

By the time Mike Wallace returned from his vacation, he was a mess. He ended up in the hospital due to emotional and physical exhaustion. During Wallace's stay at the hospital, he saw the chief of psychiatry, who officially declared that Mike Wallace was suffering from clinical depression.[3]

Actress Patty Duke, star of *The Patty Duke Show* and *The Miracle Worker,* spent many years of her life on a "wild roller coaster," as she described it, before she was properly diagnosed with manic depression, a form of clinical depression.[4] Patty Duke had gone through three marriages. One of the marriages was to a man she had met only twice. It lasted for only thirteen days. At a 1970 Emmy awards ceremony, she gave a bizarre, rambling acceptance speech that made no sense. At a press

In 1982, actress Patty Duke was diagnosed with manic depression.

conference, she flew into a rage and threatened to quit acting so she could become a doctor. At home, she would go into irrational tantrums over the slightest annoyance. She would also spend days lying in bed, crying, too depressed to take a shower and get dressed. Her sons remember banging on the bathroom door, begging their mother not to kill herself. Other days, she would go on extensive shopping sprees without a care in the world. During a manic episode, "you feel nothing you do has any kind of negative consequences . . . (you have) delusions of grandeur,"[5] Duke explains.

It was not until 1982, when her psychiatrist witnessed Duke going into a manic episode as a reaction to some medication she was taking, that he was able to finally diagnose manic depression. Before that, he had seen her only when she was depressed. (People who are manic do not usually feel that they need to see a psychiatrist.) Since then, Patty Duke has been successfully treated with lithium, the drug most commonly prescribed for manic-depressive patients.[6]

The word "depression" is commonly used in everyday conversation. People complain "I'm depressed," when they are feeling sad or down in the dumps. Everyone feels sad from time to time. It is normal to feel sad and upset when we lose a loved one, when relationships fall apart, or when we experience failure. But just feeling sad or blue does not necessarily mean you are depressed.

If you find that your depression has become continuous and has started to interfere with your everyday activities, you may suffer from *clinical depression*. This is more serious than a passing depressed mood. Clinical depression is a chronic affective disorder. "Affective" refers to the feelings or emotions, and "chronic" reflects the fact that it can go on for a long time—weeks, months, or even years.

Depression Is a Disease

Many people do not realize that depression is actually a disease. Depression is a real medical disorder, just like diabetes or cancer. According to the dictionary, disease is defined as "a condition of the living animal or plant body or of one of its parts that impairs normal functioning: sickness, malady."[7] Depression has been appropriately described as a "whole-body illness" because not only does it affect a person's mood, it can affect every aspect of a person's life. A person may suffer both emotionally and physically—from sleep disturbances to bodily aches to the destruction of relationships. Depression should be taken very seriously because it can even lead to death.

Who Suffers from Depression?

An estimated 17.6 million Americans suffer from some form of depression each year.[8] People often think of depression as a temporary situation; they do not understand the seriousness of the disorder or realize that they should seek immediate treatment.

Depression can affect anyone. It does not matter what your race is, where you live, how much money you have, or how old you are. However, depression is more common among women, occurring at twice the rate among men. Some people feel that this apparent difference between the sexes is not real, because women talk about their feelings more and are more willing to seek help. Men often keep their feelings to themselves and see depression as a sign of weakness; thus they may not seek medical aid.

It used to be believed that only adults suffer from depression, but now research has shown that children also show signs of depression. Even infants can get depressed. Studies show that infants who receive a limited amount of human contact become depressed and may even die. Adolescents are famous for being moody. But now researchers realize that some teenagers may actually be suffering from clinical depression. In fact, statistics indicate that the first episode of depression now tends to occur at an earlier age than it did in previous generations.

Depressive disorders occur most frequently in adults between the ages of twenty-five and forty-four.[9] Depression can develop in the forties and fifties (the midlife period), as well. At that time of life, a person may have to cope with many, often negative changes—declining physical strength and more frequent ailments, changes in the family structure as children grow up and leave, and perhaps the unexpected loss of a job. Depression is also a serious and growing problem among the elderly. According to estimates by the National Institute of Mental Health, 3 percent of Americans over sixty-five are clinically depressed, and from 7 to 12 percent have milder forms of depression.[10] (In some cases depression is a side effect

Children can be depressed, as well as adults. This illustration is from a medical textbook published in 1892.

of other diseases, such as diabetes, kidney or liver disorders, or heart disease; it may also be caused by medications.)

Depression is a very common illness that has a profound effect on society: estimated costs of this disease range from $16 to $45 billion each year. This includes the costs of treatment, reduced effectiveness at work or even permanent disability, and substance abuse that may develop as the depressed person searches for some way to feel better.[11]

What Are the Symptoms?

Are you feeling depressed? Have your feelings of sadness been taking over your life? How long have you been feeling this way? If a person has been experiencing symptoms of depression for longer than two weeks or there is an inability to function normally, doctors will diagnose the problem as clinical depression.

According to the *American Psychiatric Association's Diagnostic and Statistical Manual for Mental Disorders* (4th edition, 1994; also known as DSM IV), if you have at least five of the following symptoms lasting for two weeks or more, you may be clinically depressed:

- an irritable mood or feelings of sadness and grief nearly every day
- a loss of interest or pleasure in things you once enjoyed
- a change in appetite (significant weight gain or loss)
- changes in sleeping patterns (insomnia or excessive sleeping)
- physical restlessness or slowed body movements

- fatigue or loss of energy
- feelings of worthlessness or guilt
- problems in concentrating, thinking, remembering, or making decisions
- recurrent thoughts of death or suicide, or a suicide plan or attempt[12]

Symptoms of depression can vary greatly from person to person, and so can the severity and duration of symptoms. Some people may experience more symptoms than others. When a person experiences severe symptoms of depression during a given period, that period of time is known as an episode. Some people may have one episode in a lifetime, while others have recurrent episodes.

Clinical depression, like other diseases, often runs in families. Researchers believe that there are hereditary factors involved, rather than just a repetition of behavior learned from family role models. A person with a strong genetic tendency toward depression will react more severely to life's crises. The death of a loved one, divorce, or job loss can all be triggers that may dramatically alter the emotional state and behavior of such a person, leading to clinical depression. A normal person facing the same triggers may experience only feelings of sadness, without a disruption of his or her life.

What Causes Clinical Depression?

Scientists do not know exactly what causes depression. It is probably caused not by one single factor but by a combination of factors. Many scientists believe that depression is due to a chemical imbalance in the brain. Other factors may play a role as well.

Environmental factors may contribute to depression. A significant loss, a difficult relationship, or financial problems produce stress, and the body responds by secreting extra amounts of certain hormones, particularly those of the adrenal glands. Studies have shown that about one third of depressed people have enlarged adrenal glands, and many depressed people have higher-than-normal levels of the adrenal hormone cortisol. Experiments on animals have found that increased levels of stress hormones, persisting for a long time, can produce changes in the structure of the animals' brains, actually killing some of the nerve cells. These structural changes result in changes in behavior that resemble some features of clinical depression.[13]

Psychological factors may cause a person to develop a depressive illness. People whose personalities involve pessimistic thinking, low self-esteem, and excessive worrying are more likely to develop depression. These characteristics are often the result of a stressful childhood or adolescence, but some studies suggest that personality and mood are at least partly determined by heredity.

Genetic factors may thus be a cause of depression in some individuals. A family history of depression might indicate that the person has inherited a tendency toward depression. However, not everybody with a family history will develop the illness, and major depression can occur in people who have had no family members with the illness. This could mean that other factors are involved.

Biochemical factors may be another cause of clinical depression. Evidence has shown that the brain biochemistry is a significant factor in depressive disorders. For instance, people who have major depression have either too little or too much of certain brain chemicals, called neurotransmitters. However, it is not yet known if the disturbance in the release of brain chemicals is due to heredity or caused by stress, trauma, or some other environmental factors.[14]

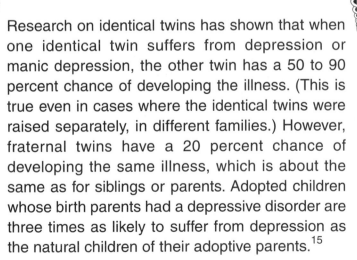

TWINS TELL THE TALE

Research on identical twins has shown that when one identical twin suffers from depression or manic depression, the other twin has a 50 to 90 percent chance of developing the illness. (This is true even in cases where the identical twins were raised separately, in different families.) However, fraternal twins have a 20 percent chance of developing the same illness, which is about the same as for siblings or parents. Adopted children whose birth parents had a depressive disorder are three times as likely to suffer from depression as the natural children of their adoptive parents.[15]

How Does the Brain Work?

Since a chemical imbalance in the brain may be responsible for many patients who are clinically depressed, it is important to understand how the brain functions and what role it plays in depression.

The nervous system, which includes our most important organ, the brain, is like a large collection of electrical wires in a complex telephone network. The brain is composed of nearly 100 billion *neurons*, or nerve cells, and other nerve cells extend out into all parts of the body. Information is transmitted throughout the entire nervous system via electrical and chemical signals that travel from one neuron to the next. Incoming signals are picked up by thin branches, called *dendrites*. Outgoing signals are transmitted by the neuron along a single long, thin strand, called an *axon*, which ends in a cluster of small branches. Unlike the wires in a telephone network, though, the axons and dendrites of the neurons in our nerve networks are not firmly connected to each other.

A message traveling from one nerve cell to another must cross a tiny, fluid-filled gap called a *synapse* between the ends of the first neuron's axon and the dendrites or main cell body of the second. Special chemicals, called *neurotransmitters*, carry the message across the synapse and spark the next neuron to "fire" in turn. Particles of a neurotransmitter chemical are released from the ends of the axon of the firing neuron, drift slowly out into the liquid that fills the gap, and cross it. They are picked up by special receptor chemicals on the surface of the next neuron in the chain. This neuron is activated in turn and fires, passing the nerve signal along. Meanwhile, its *receptors* let go of the used neurotransmitter molecules, and this chemical is recycled—reabsorbed by the nerve cell that released it, to be used the next time a signal is transmitted.

Certain neurotransmitters are known to play a role in the regulation of mood. Three particular neurotransmitters, norepinephrine, dopamine, and serotonin, are very important in depression. When the brain does not produce enough of these neurotransmitters, a disturbance in brain functioning results. Problems can also arise when the *postsynaptic neurons* (the ones to which the nerve impulses are transmitted) respond to chronic low levels of neurotransmitters by producing more receptors. This adaptation helps the brain to function more normally (the extra receptors can grab all the neurotransmitters that are available), but the neurons have become hypersensitive. They overreact when more normal levels of neurotransmitters are available, for example, if the person is being treated with an antidepressant medication. Eventually, if the higher levels continue, the postsynaptic neurons "downregulate" their sensitivity by reducing the number of receptors on the cell surface. Events that occur inside the receiving cells may also play a role. The interactions of neurons and the various kinds of neurotransmitters are very complex, and brain researchers are still proposing and testing new theories to explain them.[16]

Forms of Depression

The term *clinical depression* describes a condition in which the depression is so severe that it requires treatment. The type and severity of the symptoms are used to distinguish various forms of the disorder.

Major depression, also known as unipolar depression, is the most serious type of depressive illness. People with major depression have little or no control over their lives. In most cases, their depression does not allow them to function normally in their daily activities, like eating, sleeping, and thinking. Suicide is also more common among people who suffer from major depression. Approximately 15 percent of those who are severely depressed take their own lives.[17]

Dysthymia is a milder, chronic form of depression. Symptoms include low self-esteem, sleep disturbances, weight loss or gain, fatigue, feelings of hopelessness, and loss of concentration. Life seems flat, and the person is unable to fully enjoy good things that happen. Dysthymia is diagnosed when mild depression is present for at least two years. During that time, relief may occur intermittently, but for no more than two months at a time. People with dysthymia may also have episodes of major depression. This is called double depression.

Manic-depressive illness, also known as bipolar depression, is another form of depression. Manic-depressive illness is identified by alternating periods of highs (mania) and lows (depression). The mood changes can be sudden but are usually gradual. During a manic phase, a person may feel charged up, overflowing with ideas, and filled with energy; but then, in a depressive episode, the same person may find it difficult just to get out of bed and get dressed. The depressive phase of the

Manic depression was described by the German psychiatrist Emil Kraepelin in the early 1900s.

disorder has the same symptoms as the major depression disorder. The manic phase is dramatically different.

The following are symptoms of mania:

- extreme irritability and distractibility
- excessive "high" or euphoric feelings
- increased energy, activity, restlessness, racing thoughts, and rapid talking
- decreased need for sleep
- unrealistic beliefs in one's abilities and powers
- uncharacteristically poor judgment
- increased sexual drive
- abuse of drugs, particularly cocaine, alcohol, and sleeping medication
- obnoxious, provocative, or intrusive behavior
- denial that anything is wrong[18]

Although depression might seem to be the more serious of the two phases, the manic phase is actually more dangerous. During the manic phase, a person can stay awake for days or even weeks at a time. The manic person seems to be overflowing with energy, but all the frantic activity drains the body's reserves. Eventually the person becomes exhausted or may fall ill with an infectious disease that a healthy body could normally have fought off. In addition to the danger of physical illness, the manic person's unrealistic ideas and poor judgment can lead to spending sprees, unplanned pregnancy, or the loss of jobs and friends. The depressive phase brings a risk of suicide; a manic episode can wreck a person's life.

Manic-depressive illness might seem to be a completely different disease from major depression, but many studies have shown that both types typically are found in various members of the same family. Major depression that occurs in cycles might be regarded as a sort of variation of bipolar disorder, in which depressive phases occur but manic episodes do not.

Seasonal affective disorder (SAD) is another type of depression. People who suffer from SAD usually experience the symptoms of major depression, but only during the fall and winter months when there is decreased sunlight because of the shortened days. Scientists believe that people have a kind of internal biological clock that runs according to schedules for a twenty-four-hour period, which are called *circadian rhythms*. These rhythms are usually adjusted by the daily changes of the light-dark cycle. Everyone has his or her own internal schedule that regulates body temperature, blood pressure, hormonal secretions, sleep and activity cycles, and many other bodily functions. The body is normally able to adjust and synchronize to the changing environmental rhythms, such as the longer and shorter days of summer and winter. However, SAD patients have a malfunction in their circadian rhythms, and this throws off their "body clock."

Scientists believe that a seasonal disturbance in the cycling of *melatonin* causes the body clock to malfunction. Melatonin is a hormone secreted into the bloodstream by the pineal gland, a small structure deep inside the brain. This hormone allows the body to adjust to the light and dark of the day and night. Some people's body cycles seem to be out of sync with the normal daily rhythms, causing their internal clocks to run a few hours behind or ahead of schedule. Some people are

French psychiatrist Jean Etienne Esquirol identified seasonal affective disorder in the 1800s.

ANOTHER SIDE OF SAD

Researchers have recently discovered another side of seasonal affective disorder. People with SAD usually become depressed during the fall and winter months, but some people actually become depressed during the spring and summer months instead. The explanation for the "summertime blues" is not quite clear. Researchers have theorized that it may be caused by a combination of heat, humidity, and possibly the intense, glaring light of summer. Since temperature seems to be a factor, treatment is a bit more complicated than the light therapy being used for those who experience "wintertime blues."[19]

night owls, for example, who hit their peak efficiency late in the day, are still wide awake late at night, and find it difficult to get up in the morning. Medical researchers have discovered that these patients can be treated successfully with artificial-light therapy.[20]

Determining that a case of the blues is actually a serious, clinical depression is the first step toward getting effective medical help. Pinpointing the type of depression—diagnosing the condition—can be an important key to regaining a normal zest for life.

Diagnosis

Janet was a smart, quiet girl who was well liked by her friends and her teachers. In junior high, she started to have trouble paying attention in class, but no one thought much about it. After all, everyone at that age gets a little restless. In high school, Janet did rather poorly, but since she was not a troublemaker, the teachers left her alone and figured she just was not interested in school. Janet's parents were a bit concerned, but no one seemed to take her poor behavior seriously. Janet saw the school counselor, who assured her parents that it was just a normal part of adolescence, and she would eventually outgrow her problems.

That was not the case. Janet's problems seemed to be getting worse. Before her senior year, Janet felt as though she could not even get out of bed in the morning. Once she finally did get up, she could not get herself motivated to do anything.

Janet lost her appetite, she could not sleep, and she could not stop crying.

Finally, Janet's parents realized that this was not just a part of growing up and they took her to the family doctor. The physician referred them to a mood disorders clinic. After taking a clinical analysis of Janet's behavior, the doctor at the clinic came to the conclusion that Janet suffered from clinical depression. The doctor immediately prescribed an antidepressant. Within a month, Janet's behavior was much better. In fact, she made new friends, and her schoolwork improved dramatically. She could not remember the last time she had felt so good.[1]

No Longer an Adult Disease

Diagnosing clinical depression has changed a great deal over the years. For a long time people thought that severe depression was an illness that affected only adults. Psychiatrist Frederick K. Goodwin at the National Institute of Mental Health explains:

> Adolescents didn't develop "real" depression—they just had "adolescent adjustment problems," so most psychiatrists didn't and still don't think to look for it in kids. Now, however, we know that idea is dead wrong. Adolescents, even children, suffer from major depression as much as adults do.[2]

In fact, this problem appears to be increasing. According to one study, in the past forty years there has been a fivefold increase in the percentage of older teenagers with major affective disorders.[3] Doctors are able to diagnose teenage depression more accurately these days, which may have contributed to the dramatic increase in statistics over the years.

Collecting Information

Unlike many other diseases, depression cannot be identified by a simple blood test. The key to a proper diagnosis is to collect information from the patient. According to the DSM IV, diagnosing depression is based on the symptoms that were described in the previous chapter. A list of the patient's symptoms is then classified as mild, moderate, or severe. The doctor is then able to categorize the severity and type of depression: major depression, manic depression, SAD, or dysthymia.

Determining the symptoms of the illness is very important, but the doctor needs to collect more information from the patient before a proper diagnosis can be made. A complete history must be taken from the patient. This includes five categories:

1. *A developmental history.* This type of history goes back to the beginning—birth. How was the mother's pregnancy? Was it a normal delivery? Did the child start crawling, walking, talking, and toilet training at the appropriate ages?

2. *A medical history.* Was the child healthy as an infant and toddler? Or was there some chronic medical condition,

allergies, or repeated ear and respiratory infections? Accidents, surgery, and hospitalizations may be significant. (Many depressed children have a history of illness during their early years.)

3. *A psychological history.* What is the child's temperament: easygoing or difficult, outgoing or shy? Did the child have temper tantrums? Were there any pronounced fears or phobias?

4. *An educational history.* Children who are depressed often have a history of poor performance in school. Many children have problems paying attention in class.

5. *A family history.* The relationship between family members can have an effect on the child's emotional state of mind. The doctor should also be informed about any mood and anxiety disorders, alcoholism, and learning disabilities in the family background going back to the grandparents.[4]

Physical Examination

Patients should have a routine physical examination, as well as blood tests, urinalysis, and an electrocardiogram (EKG). These tests are very important because they can rule out any medical reasons for their depression.[5]

Thorough testing is especially important in the case of elderly patients, who may exhibit signs of depression in the form of physical symptoms such as headaches, backaches, digestive problems, or insomnia. Common symptoms of

There is no simple test to diagnose depression. Here, a psychiatrist is listening to a patient's reactions to a problem picture.

depression such as memory lapses or difficulty in concentrating may be mistaken in elderly patients as symptoms of Alzheimer's disease, or dismissed as normal parts of the aging process.[6]

Psychological Tests

Psychological tests, often used for children, can be a very helpful tool in giving additional information about the patient. These tests, which include the Rorschach ink-blot test and the thematic apperception test, involve interpreting pictures that are shown. This can tell a lot about a person's own needs, fears, and struggles. However, some professionals do not recommend this approach because it is time-consuming and costly. They also feel that the same information can be obtained through the clinical interview.[7]

Medical Laboratory Tests

There are presently no laboratory tests that will actually identify clinical depression. However, researchers are in the process of developing and improving various diagnostic tests. Although these experimental tests are not scientifically proven, some are more effective than others.

One diagnostic test is called the *dexamethasone suppression test (DST)*. This test is based on the observation that during an episode of depression there are increased levels of cortisol, a hormone secreted by the adrenal gland. The adrenal glands, located on top of each kidney, secrete hormones as a coping response to stress. However, this test is not generally scientifically accepted, because it identifies only about 45 to 50 percent of depressed adults.[8]

Another diagnostic test is the *sleep electroencephalogram (EEG)*, which measures brain electrical activity during sleep. Researchers have discovered that patients who suffer from major depression have different sleep patterns from normal. Depressed patients enter the dreaming phase of sleep more quickly, but do not sleep as deeply or as long as nondepressed people. The test is usually taken in a specialized laboratory with the patient sleeping, which can take up to three nights. Therefore, this test can be very expensive, making it unavailable in many areas.[9]

Various types of scanners, which provide pictures of the inner structures of the brain, are being used experimentally and may provide more reliable diagnostic tests in the future. One type is *magnetic resonance imaging (MRI)*. The nuclei of different types of atoms send out characteristic signals under the influence of a magnetic field. Mapping the signals of atoms in key compounds, such as water or ATP (a chemical the body uses to store energy), yields a detailed image of a "slice" of the brain without damaging it.

Positron emission tomography (PET) is another type of medical imaging, which makes it possible to observe which parts of the brain are active. In PET, a glucose solution "tagged" with atoms that emit very active particles, called positrons, is injected into the body. This solution is absorbed by the body's active brain cells, which emit positrons. Researchers are trying to find patterns of brain activity characteristic of people with depression.

Diagnosing clinical depression is a very complex process that cannot be completed in a single meeting. The process can be time-consuming and expensive. The situation is complicated by the need to rule out other disorders and choose a diagnostic test that is right for the particular patient. There are no foolproof diagnostic tests. However, the person must be properly diagnosed before an effective treatment plan can be implemented.

5

Treatment

Psychologist Dr. Howard treated Beth, a teenager who suffered from depression. Beth admitted that, most of the time, she felt like she was in a daze and rarely enjoyed herself because she was so used to being sad all the time. Beth had poor self-esteem. She often felt that no one cared about her—not her family or her friends. She also found herself overreacting to everyday situations. Dr. Howard asked Beth to keep a journal and write in it every day about the things that made her get overly emotional. By analyzing the situations that made Beth very upset, as recorded in her journal, Dr. Howard hoped to find out what was triggering Beth's depression.

In her journal, Beth complained of days when she was feeling really miserable and she did not even know why. When she got upset, she would take it out on her friends. This angered them and resulted in many arguments. Beth felt her friends did not understand her and did not share her values. Beth was so desperate for help that she asked Dr. Howard to put her on an antidepressant. Dr. Howard recommended Zoloft and phoned Beth's doctor for a prescription. He told her it would take a few weeks before the drug would work. In the meantime, things did not get any easier for Beth. She seemed to cry constantly. One day Beth found out that her brother and his twelve-year-old friends had messed up her room. Suddenly, Beth lost control of her emotions and her body. Screaming uncontrollably, she ran into the kitchen and cut her hand with a knife. Beth's mother and brother were both very shaken by what they had seen.

The next day Dr. Howard told her not to physically harm herself again or she might need to stay in a hospital for a couple of weeks for therapy. Dr. Howard told her that she needed to practice her positive thinking when she found herself in a potentially upsetting situation. After a few weeks of taking Zoloft, Beth thought the medicine was finally starting to work. Her mind was clearer and she was now able to think more positively than before. She would still get sad from time to time, but she did not cry as much anymore. She also started to care more about things.

Beth still had some problems with being overly sensitive to jokes that her friends made. But Beth continued to think positively, and she was finally getting better at putting a lid on her temper. She was now able to have a good time with her friends. Dr. Howard was proud of Beth's success. However, he recommended that Beth take Zoloft for three more months because it would take about six months with the drug in her system to stabilize her chemical imbalance.

When Beth had her last session with Dr. Howard, she could not believe she was finally going to be independent. In the last entry of her journal, Beth wrote some thoughtful words about her recovery: "I've opened the heavy door of darkness and stepped back into the world of light."[1]

Depression is a very treatable disease. Treatment can reduce symptoms in over 80 percent of depressed patients.[2] However, it is clear that we still do not have the perfect treatment for clinical depression. Drug treatment is a very individualized process. What may seem like a miracle for one person may be very dangerous to another. Therefore, doctors try to offer as many options as possible, to see which treatment works the best for each patient's particular situation.

Mood-Altering Drugs

Antidepressant drugs are often called mood elevators. When people are feeling low, antidepressants can elevate their mood to a more normal level. But these drugs are not "happy pills." They do not make users walk around with silly grins on their faces. However, too high a dose of the medication might elevate a person's mood to unhealthy levels.[3] (It is therefore important for a doctor to monitor any antidepressant drug treatment program.)

Antidepressant drugs are actually mood regulators. The purpose of these drugs is to restore the patient's mood to normal functioning by correcting the chemical imbalance in the brain. They work by changing the concentration of the neurotransmitters, the chemicals that carry messages from one neuron to another. Some drugs increase the amount of neurotransmitters available by blocking their reuptake—reabsorption by the nerve cells that released them, after they had transmitted the signal to the next neuron. Other drugs block the action of an enzyme called *monoamine oxidase,* which breaks down neurotransmitters.

The first antidepressant drugs were not very specific. They acted on the levels not only of norepinephrine and serotonin, the neurotransmitters believed to be most involved in depression, but also on other neurotransmitters such as histamine and acetylcholine. As a result, they have a number of side effects, which can be rather annoying. Imipramine and related drugs, for example, can cause sweating, irregular heartbeat, dry mouth, and constipation. These side effects result from a decrease in acetylcholine secretion, which is normally a part of the body's reaction to emergencies.[4] Other common side effects include blurred vision and drowsiness. Some of the newer drugs are more specific in their action and thus produce fewer and milder side effects. For example, fluoxetine, better known by its brand name, Prozac, acts only on the reuptake of serotonin and does not affect the levels of other neurotransmitters.[5]

Patients must take their medication continuously in order for the treatment to work correctly. It usually takes three to six weeks before the medication becomes effective. Eight weeks of

CARBO BINGEING

Mental health specialists have observed that many people who are depressed tend to eat a lot of carbohydrate-rich foods, such as pasta, bread, potatoes, chips, and candy. Part of the reason may be purely psychological—the person is unconsciously seeking comfort from familiar foods associated with happy times of childhood. But there is also a possible biochemical explanation. Carbohydrate-rich foods stimulate the production of the neurotransmitter serotonin and thus may help to elevate a person's mood.[6]

In the case of chocolate, there is an additional factor. Chocolate contains several mood-affecting drugs, including the stimulants theobromine and caffeine and a neurotransmitter called beta-phenylethylamine (PEA). This chemical acts on the brain to produce feelings of euphoria; studies have shown, in fact, that increased amounts of PEA are secreted in the brain when a person falls in love![7]

treatment are needed to decide if a drug is not working. The doctor will prescribe a different drug if the medication is not suitable for the patient. About a third of the patients stop taking prescribed drugs because of side effects. When an effective treatment for the patient has been found, the medication is usually continued for at least a few months after the depression has lifted.[8]

Tricyclic antidepressants have been used for nearly forty years. They were named for their chemical structure, which includes three rings of carbon atoms. These drugs have proven to be most effective for adults and children who suffer from moderate to severe depression. The tricyclics most commonly prescribed for children are imipramine (Tofranil) and desipramine (Norpramin).

Monoamine oxidase inhibitors (MAOIs) are another type of antidepressant. A major disadvantage of MAOIs is that patients who take them must avoid foods rich in the amino acid tyramine; the list of forbidden foods includes aged cheese, processed meats, wine, and beer. This would be difficult for those who find it hard to resist treats like pepperoni pizza or beer and wine when out with their friends. Nasal decongestants and cough medicines should also be avoided. Failing to follow the rules can have dire results, ranging from headache, chest pain, and vomiting to severely elevated blood pressure—and even the risk of death from brain hemorrhage! For these reasons, MAOIs are not very popular drugs these days and are usually used only for treating adult patients who are severely depressed. The MAOI drugs most commonly prescribed are isocarboxazid (Marplan), phenelzine (Nardil), and tranylcypromine (Parnate).

Selective serotonin re-uptake inhibitors (SSRIs) are the newest of the drugs used to treat depression. Among these is the most famous antidepressant, fluoxetine (Prozac). Other SSRIs include sertraline (Zoloft) and paroxetine (Paxil).

The major advantage of SSRIs is that they have minimal side effects. Prozac has proven to be safe and effective for children and adolescents, as well as adults. Prozac has become so popular that many consider it a miracle drug. However, others are convinced that Prozac is a mind-altering drug that causes people to act out violently and do things they would not normally do. In fact, people have tried to use Prozac as a defense in the courtroom to explain their outrageous behavior. So far, Prozac has not been proven to be an acceptable defense in a courtroom. This drug has also been accused of producing suicidal thoughts. Some experts believe, however, that the person was already considering suicide but was too depressed to act until the drug began to have a mood-lifting effect.

Because of the bad publicity that Prozac has received over the years, some people who could be helped by this drug are too afraid to use it. Yet, studies have repeatedly shown that it is one of the safest and most effective of all the antidepressants. However, as with any medication, some people may find success with Prozac or other SSRIs, while others may not.

Lithium is the drug most commonly prescribed to treat manic-depressive disorder. The effects of lithium are remarkable—80 percent of manic-depressive adults treated with lithium showed a great improvement of symptoms. Lithium works mainly to control manic episodes, but it can help to break the whole bipolar cycle and thus prevent depressive episodes as well. However, lithium treatment should be closely monitored by a physician, since too much could be toxic.[9]

Psychotherapy

Psychotherapy, sometimes called "the talking cure," is another option for treating mood disorders. Psychotherapy involves a wide variety of techniques that help people to change their attitudes, emotions, and behavior patterns. The goal of *insight-oriented therapy* is to bring buried conflicts to the person's conscious awareness. After gaining insight into this material, the person learns how to confront and master the sources of conflict so that he or she can get past them.

Sigmund Freud, known as the father of psychoanalysis, is responsible for most of the theories involved in insight-oriented therapy. According to Freud's psychoanalytic theory, the symptoms of depression and anxiety are caused by an inner struggle against unacceptable sexual and aggressive impulses or pressure from buried memories of traumatic experiences such as separation from the mother, death or loss of a loved one, sexual overstimulation, or great physical pain and suffering. Since these impulses and memories are too terrible to face, they become repressed, that is, hidden from conscious awareness, to protect the person from unbearable pain. But the repressed impulses and memories continue to

Sigmund Freud, the father of psychoanalysis, is shown here in a portrait taken in 1922.

work on the unconscious mind, producing conflict that may produce symptoms of psychological distress.

Cognitive therapy is one of the most effective types of therapy for depressed patients. Dr. Aaron Beck, the psychiatrist who did the groundbreaking work on this technique, believed that people who think negatively about themselves, the world, and the future will develop feelings of depression and despair. The goal of cognitive therapy is to analyze the patient's present way of thinking and then change the negative, nonproductive thoughts. Here are some of the ways that patients can improve their thought processes:

1. The patient should try to change every negative statement into a positive statement.

2. Depressed people have a tendency to blame themselves for the bad things that happen to them, but explain their achievements or successes by saying that they "got lucky." They need to take responsibility for the good things that happen as well as the bad.

3. Patients need to monitor their negative ways of thinking and to reward themselves when they consciously change that pattern.

Interpersonal psychotherapy is a very effective method for treating depression, even though treatment is usually brief, often lasting only twelve to sixteen weeks. This technique is based on the idea that individuals become depressed because of the problems that arise within the person's relationship with family or friends. These problems—such as grieving over the

In this 1910 caricature, Sigmund Freud is shown analyzing a figure of himself lying on a couch talking about his dreams, which are filled with symbolic images.

loss of a loved one, life changes like starting a new school or job, constant fighting between family members or friends, and a negative outlook and putting others down—put a strain on relationships. The therapist helps patients learn new ways of behaving that would improve their communication skills and relationships with others.

Family therapy is another method of treatment that can benefit depressed individuals. This technique involves bringing the entire family together for the session, to work on specific problem areas. For instance, children may feel depressed because their parents are having marital problems. The goal is to identify the source of trouble in the family, improve communication between all family members, and learn problem-solving skills.

Behavioral therapy is based on the idea that depression is a learned behavior. People learn to behave in certain ways in order to receive a reward or avoid a punishment. For instance, a young child learns to say please if the reward is a cookie. If the behavior produces no effects or has negative consequences, then the behavior quickly diminishes. Behavior therapy usually focuses on symptoms of problems, such as overeating, and it is most effective when the problem is clearly defined.

Drug treatment may be effective for some depressed patients, while psychological treatment may work well for others. However, most experts agree that the best treatment for depression is a combination of drug and psychological therapies. Medication can work on the biological aspect of the

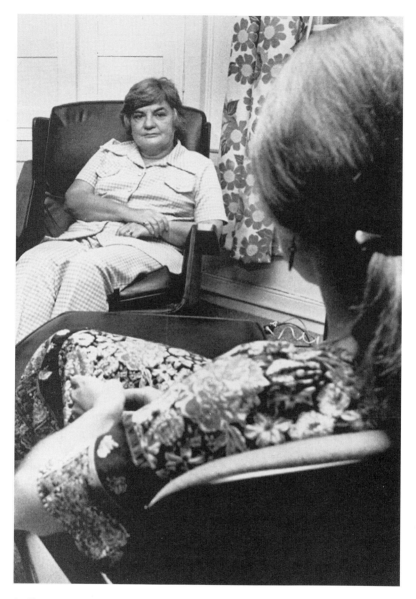

Talking it out: Dr. Chislaine Godenne, Director of Counseling and Psychiatric Services at Johns Hopkins University, is shown here in a session with a student.

disorder so that the person can work on the psychological aspect.[10]

Alternative Treatments

In the 1980s, researchers discovered that patients with seasonal affective disorder could be treated effectively by using bright artificial light. *Light therapy* involves specially designed light boxes, which produce up to ten thousand lux (twenty times brighter than the light in an average living room). When patients are exposed to this light for at least thirty minutes each day, after a few days they may experience improved mood, improved concentration, and newfound energy.[11]

When a patient's depression is so severe that he or she does not respond to any medication or psychotherapy, the doctor may prescribe electroconvulsive therapy, also known as "shock therapy." People tend to fear ECT because they have a frightening image in their mind: A person is strapped to a table; electrodes are attached to the person's head, sending volts of electricity into the brain; and the person screams in pain, like the heroine in *The Snake Pit*. Although this image was once true, ECT is now actually a safe, painless procedure. The patient is comfortably sedated during the procedure and closely monitored throughout. However, because books and movies tend to perpetuate the negative stereotypes of shock therapy, society still thinks of ECT as barbaric. Actually, ECT can be very effective in treating severely depressed patients.

The objective of electroconvulsive therapy is to produce convulsions (seizures) to treat mood disorders. This idea was developed when it was observed that some patients who suffered from both epilepsy and depression showed dramatic improvement in psychiatric symptoms after a seizure. Doctors then devised a method that involved using large doses of insulin to produce seizures in severely depressed patients. These patients showed remarkable improvements. However, using large doses of insulin proved to be rather dangerous, so they switched to a much safer method of producing a seizure—delivering an electrical current to the brain by small electrodes pasted on the skin of the head.[12]

TV personality Dick Cavett suffered years of severe depression. It took control of his whole life until it seemed that his only hope was ECT. Cavett said that people have an image of "someone standing in a tub of water and putting his finger in a socket," but it was nothing like that. For him, ECT was miraculous. Cavett described ECT as a "jump starter" that gets you "back among the living."[13] Although many people find ECT very effective and even "miraculous," as Dick Cavett puts it, ECT should remain an important option, but should be used only as a last resort. Doctors administer ECT generally to severely depressed patients and only under very controlled conditions. ECT does have its drawbacks. Some of the problems with ECT include memory loss, confusion, disorientation, and anxiety. Although these problems usually clear up within a few hours or days, memory loss may last up to a couple of months.

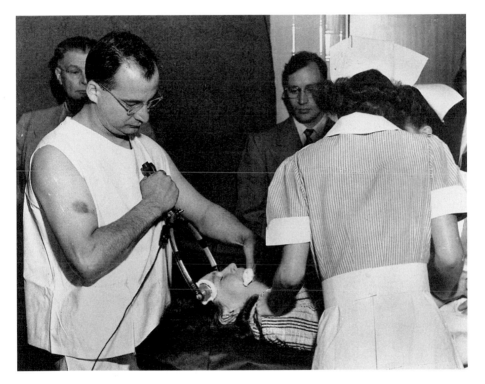

Electroshock therapy is shown here being administered at Western State Hospital in 1949.

Hospitalization

Sometimes it may be necessary to admit a depressed person into a psychiatric hospital. The decision for hospitalization can be very difficult and very complicated. Although most such individuals can be treated as outpatients, sometimes the person is aggressive or suicidal and thus is a danger to him- or herself or to others. When a child or teenager is clinically depressed, the family may become overwhelmed and unable to cope with the problem alone. A hospital can provide a safe environment to help the patient through the crisis. The controlled routine of the hospital, together with intensive, carefully monitored treatment—away from a home environment that may have been adding to the problems— can often bring the patient more quickly to a more stable condition.

In a psychiatric hospital depressed patients can get the attention they deserve. The hospital staff can monitor the patients at all times and make sure they are taking the proper dosage of medication. Manic-depressives, for example, sometimes do not take their lithium regularly on their own—especially when they are manic. (They may feel so good that they do not think they need any medication; or they may resent the drug that brings them back to reality.) In addition, the hospital staff is trained to handle emergencies and can protect patients from injuring themselves or others.[14]

Hospitalization is not always voluntary, even when the person needs help desperately. For instance, manic-depressives often deny that they have a problem when they are in their manic phase. They think that since they are feeling so good, they do not need help. Sometimes it may be necessary to admit them against their will. But laws protecting people's rights make it very difficult to do this unless it can be clearly established that the person is suicidal or has made violent threats against others.

◆ ◆ ◆ ◆ ◆

Thus, there are various types of treatment available to people with affective disorders. Unfortunately, choosing the most effective one is not an easy task. Although finding the right treatment is very important, people can also help to improve their condition by reducing stress in their lives, which will remove additional triggers of depression.

6

Prevention

Every day, people are faced with life's problems. Some problems are more serious than others—and people react to them differently. People who suffer from depression typically have a more difficult time dealing with the stresses of daily living than other people do. It is the combination of an inherited predisposition and extreme stress that may trigger an episode of clinical depression. So people who have suffered from depression in the past, or who have family members who have problems with depression, may be able to reduce their number of depressive episodes by being aware of potential stresses and of their own reactions to them. Self-awareness can also make them alert to the early signs of clinical depression and allow them to seek help promptly.

Since depression may be caused by biochemical or genetic factors, it can take a great deal of desire and determination to keep that black cloud from hovering overhead. Serious changes need to be made in the person's lifestyle and outlook. There are numerous ways that a person can try to lessen or even eliminate the negative effects of stress.

The first step is to identify the various life stresses. The following are some stressful situations that may be experienced by college students. They are listed in order from the most stressful to the least stressful. How many have you experienced, and how did you react?

- death of a spouse
- unwanted pregnancy
- death of a parent
- father in an unwanted pregnancy
- divorce
- death of a close relative
- death of a close friend
- parents' divorce
- jail term
- major injury or illness
- flunking out of school
- marriage
- loss of a job
- loss of financial aid
- failing an important course
- sexual difficulties
- argument with a partner
- academic probation
- change in major field of study
- new love interest
- increased workload
- outstanding achievement

- first semester
- conflict with instructor
- lower grades than expected
- college transfer
- change in social activities
- change in sleeping habits
- change in eating habits
- minor violations of the law[1]

A few of the items in that list are actually positive things. But any change in the daily routine, whether positive or negative, can be considered stressful—and stress is often a key factor in the development of affective disorders.

There are various ways to deal with stresses without letting them affect you emotionally or physically.

First, when you are faced with a stressful situation, take a deep breath. Slowly inhale through your nose and then slowly exhale. Deep breathing can actually lower your blood pressure and pulse rate.

Exercise is a great way to work off nervous energy. It can even help you feel good about yourself. It does not take much time—a twenty-minute walk a few times a week can have health and relaxation benefits. Also, doing exercises specifically to relax your muscles can be very helpful. The parts of the body that are under the most tension are the neck, the shoulders, the jaw, and the back.

Meditation is also helpful in lowering the heart rate, blood pressure, and stress-hormone level. Using your imagination to create soothing scenery in your mind can also help you to relax.

Eat a healthy diet and do not skip meals. This can help you to feel your best, and it will keep you from running out of energy during the day. Also, chewing can actually release tension in your jaw muscles.

Get a good night's sleep. This will allow you to feel refreshed when you wake up, ready to tackle the day.

Pets can be good stress relievers. In 1991 a study of eight thousand people at Monash University in Melbourne, Australia, showed that pet owners had lower blood pressure than those without pets. Talking to your pets keeps you from thinking about yourself and all the things you need to do.

Write down your problems in a journal. This can help you to sort them out and make them more manageable and understandable.

Screen your calls so you can have some time for yourself.

Do your shopping during off-hours when there are no long lines. Waiting in line can be a big stressor.

Draw up a realistic budget. Excessive credit-card debt and bank loans can create a great deal of stress and tension.

Set aside some time in the day to talk with your family to develop better communication among all members. Also tape TV shows to watch when it is more convenient, so you can spend some quality time with your family.

Make plans to go out and see a movie or go out to dinner. This gives you something to look forward to.

You need to speak up. Do not let people take advantage of you. Learn how to say no sometimes. This will relieve your anger and frustration, and you will feel better about yourself.

The idea that humor can help handle stress and relieve depression is not new. In this illustration from a book published in 1670, actors are trying to cheer up a melancholy scholar.

Talk to someone about your problems, whether it be a good friend, a family member, or a counselor. Keeping your anger and frustrations to yourself can be very unhealthy, both emotionally and physically.

Worrying about everything is a waste of energy. Can you control what you are worrying about? If not, then do not waste your time.

Procrastinating can be very stressful. By putting things off, you spend all your time worrying about them. But when the job is done right away, there is no more reason to get all worked up over it.

Do not be too hard on yourself if you do not succeed at something. The need for perfection can cause a lot of unnecessary stress. Nobody is perfect.

Finally, one of the best ways to handle stress is a good sense of humor. Laughter really is the best medicine. According to Joel Goodman, director of the Humor Project in Saratoga Springs, New York: "Research shows that laughing inhibits stress hormones, and studies have shown that people with a good sense of humor are more successful without being more stressed."[2]

Finding ways to avoid stress and learning how to deal with stressful situations are helpful. However, since depression is often caused by a genetic predisposition, depression cannot always be prevented even by the most motivated individual. Therefore, seeking professional help may sometimes be the best solution for those who are clinically depressed.

7

Depression and Society

T he noted artist Vincent Van Gogh came from a family of people who showed evidence of mental illness. Of his four siblings, three suffered from mental disorders and one committed suicide. The artist himself suffered from devastating mood swings. He felt lonely and unloved, and he actually turned to art as an adult, after failing at every other career he attempted. In his paintings Van Gogh was able to pour out his troubled feelings, but in this career, too, he failed to receive the respect he craved—he sold only one painting during his lifetime! All these life stresses were overwhelming for someone who already had a tendency toward an affective disorder. But Van Gogh did not suffer just from depressive episodes; his mood disorder was bipolar. The bizarre incident that Van Gogh is so famous for—cutting off his ear after a violent argument with his friend, Paul Gauguin—may have been

The artist, Vincent Van Gogh, shown in this self-portrait, suffered from manic-depressive illness.

prompted by his manic-depressive illness. During his manic phase, Van Gogh's bursts of energy often filled him with creative ideas for paintings. Some of his best work was created while he was experiencing mania. In fact, while Van Gogh was staying in Auvers-sur-Oise, France, he painted seventy pictures in the same number of days. Finally, Van Gogh lost his battle with his destructive disorder when he committed suicide in 1890.[1]

Vincent Van Gogh was not alone in his struggle with the severe mood swings of manic-depressive disorder. Throughout history, many other talented artists have suffered the same illness. They include the poets Edgar Allan Poe, Lord Byron, and Alfred Lord Tennyson; the novelists Virginia Woolf and Samuel Clemens (Mark Twain); the playwright Tennessee Williams; and the composer Robert Schumann. Their paintings, poems, writings, and music all revealed the extreme mood swings they endured.

The Creativity Link

Scientists believe that there is a connection between creativity and manic-depressive illness. In fact, recent studies revealed that during the manic phase of the disorder, people tend to be more creative than usual. Creative people are often very sensitive, independent, and intelligent. What sets them apart from the rest of the world is the ability to see things in a whole different light, which allows them to convey these visions through their music, paintings, poetry, or theater. When creative people become manic, their minds are overflowing with thoughts and ideas, which, in turn, can be used constructively in their artwork. Heightened senses and a lack of the normal inhibitions may allow them to produce unique and imaginative works of art.

Dr. Kay Redfield Jamison, a psychologist at the Johns Hopkins University School of Medicine, explains the creativity link:

> Their associations are genuinely unusual. And having extremes of emotion is a gift—the capacity to be passionately involved in life, to care deeply about things, to feel hurt: a lot of people don't have that. And it is the transition in and out of the highs and lows, the constant contrast, that can foster creativity.[2]

(Mania is sometimes romanticized among creative people, but it should not be taken lightly since it can be very destructive.)

In 1987, psychiatrist Nancy J. C. Andreasen revealed the results of a fifteen-year study designed to investigate the connection between creativity and manic depression. The study focused on a group of creative writers on the faculty of the University of Iowa Writers' Workshop. They were compared with a control group of lawyers, hospital administrators, and social workers, who would not be considered creative. Dr. Andreasen found that 80 percent of the writers had suffered at least one episode of depression or mania in their lifetime, compared to only 30 percent of the lawyers, hospital administrators, and social workers.[3]

Other studies supported Dr. Andreasen's findings about creativity and manic depression. Dr. Kay Redfield Jamison conducted a similar study at Oxford University and St. George's Hospital in London. The study involved forty-seven highly regarded British artists and writers. The study revealed that about one third had a history of severe mood disorders (with 63 percent of the playwrights and more than 50 percent of the poets having sought treatment); all of the poets, novelists, and artists, and 88 percent of the playwrights recalled episodes of intense creative highs, when they were filled with ideas and energy, needed less sleep, and felt that their thoughts were flowing faster and more easily than usual.[4]

Depression and Drug Abuse

Research has shown that there is a strong link between mood disorders and substance abuse. The National Institute of Mental Health (NIMH) reports that alcohol and cocaine abuse is significantly more common among people with mood disorders, especially manic-depressive disorder. In addition, a family history of alcoholism is not uncommon. However, mood disorders and substance abuse often occur together, and their symptoms are very similar: euphoria, grandiose feelings, impairment of judgment, staying up all night, and irritability. Therefore, doctors may have a difficult time choosing a primary diagnosis: manic depression, alcoholism, or drug abuse. According to the NIMH, 60 percent of manic-depressive patients are also diagnosed with drug or alcohol abuse, giving them a dual diagnosis.

Initially, manic-depressive patients may use drugs or alcohol as a form of self-treatment, to dull their emotional pain. People with affective disorders feel depressed or agitated more often than normal people. Therefore, it is understandable that they often turn to drugs or alcohol to give them a boost when they are depressed, or calm them down when they are agitated. However, eventually the drugs or alcohol start to aggravate the symptoms rather than help them. The drugs act on neurotransmitters in the brain, at first stimulating and then overstimulating the nerve-cell pathways involved in emotions and mood. Ultimately they damage the natural control systems, and the person then experiences even more mood changes.[5]

Depression and Suicide

Suicide is a very complex behavior. A combination of risk factors, which may include depression, other mental disorders, and addictions, may lead to thoughts of suicide, suicide attempts, and committing suicide. Severe depression seems to be a very common component of suicidal behavior. It is understandable that when people suffer from depressive disorders, thoughts of hopelessness and despair become overwhelming, making them feel alone and vulnerable. In fact, adults with depressive illness are thirty times more likely than others in the population to commit suicide.

Unfortunately, adolescents who suffer from depression also have a significant risk for suicidal behavior. In fact, suicide is the third leading cause of death among young people fifteen to twenty-four years of age. Some studies show startling statistics—as many as 11 percent of all high school students admit to having made at least one suicide attempt, and an estimated twelve thousand children from five to twelve years old have thought about or attempted suicide.[6] Although children and adolescents have the lowest suicide rates of any age group, studies show that the rate has recently increased somewhat.

The strongest risk factors for suicide in teenagers are depression, alcohol or other drug use disorder, and aggressive behaviors. Scientific research shows that recognition and appropriate treatment of substance abuse and mental disorders, including depression, is the best way to prevent suicide and suicidal behavior.

Major risk factors for suicidal behavior:[7]

Previous suicide attempt—Often viewed as a "cry for help," a suicide attempt should be taken seriously. It is highly possible that a teenager who has tried suicide in the past may try suicide again—but this time it could be fatal (even if the original intention was just a try for attention).

Substance abuse—Alcohol and drugs often play a role in suicide. They impair people's judgment, making them wide open for any type of danger. Since drugs and alcohol lower inhibitions, impulsive behavior becomes more likely. In addition, since alcohol is a depressant, it tends to intensify feelings of depression and anger, making suicide seem like a good option to troubled teenagers looking for a way out of their emotional turmoil.

Coexisting psychiatric conditions—Teenagers who steal, fight, or run away from home are also likely to abuse alcohol and drugs. Therefore, this puts them at serious risk for suicidal behavior. People with a psychiatric condition called borderline personality disorder have unstable relationships with others, extreme mood changes, and difficulties in controlling intense anger. Trying to escape from feelings of emptiness and boredom, they engage in risky and irresponsible activities such as reckless driving, spending sprees, casual sex, substance abuse, and shoplifting. Their destructive behavior greatly increases the risk of suicide.

Dysfunctional family—Suicidal teenagers often come from families where there is a great deal of conflict among family members. The parents are often involved with their own problems and do not make themselves available to their children. They lack communication and problem-solving skills.

Family history of suicide—Like depression, suicide "runs in families." Teenagers are more likely to engage in suicidal behavior if a relative has committed suicide, especially a parent. It is difficult to say if this is due to heredity or environment. It may be a little of both. When a parent commits suicide, the child may become depressed, which can lead to suicide.

But there is evidence for hereditary causes, too. Research has found that suicidal people are likely to have abnormalities in the way their brains manufacture and use the neurotransmitter serotonin. Low levels of 5-HIAA, a chemical substance that results from the breakdown of serotonin, have been found in the spinal fluid of many people who have attempted violent suicide. Neuroscientists have recently located a gene that is involved in this process.[8]

Poor social relationships—Teenagers who have difficulty making friends or getting along with others are more likely to be depressed and possibly even suicidal. Adolescence is a time when peer relationships are very important. Teenagers who lack social skills may feel alone and are unable to find any support in their time of need.

The presence of a firearm in the home—Suicide is often an impulsive act and is much more likely to be attempted—and to be successful—when a gun is readily available in the home. Some researchers have found that even after a child has made one or more attempts at suicide, parents typically do not get rid of the guns in the home.[9]

Stressful life events—Teenagers who have traumatic experiences, such as physical or sexual abuse or the loss of a parent through death or divorce, are at a higher-than-normal risk for suicide. Being arrested, breaking up with a girl- or boyfriend, having to take an important test (or failing one), or moving to a new school can cause extreme anxiety that may lead to a suicide attempt. In a study of 120 young New Yorkers who committed suicide, Dr. David Shaffer, a researcher at Columbia University College of Physicians and Surgeons, found that "most killed themselves within a few hours of either expecting trouble or getting into trouble." Dr.

Shaffer points out that similar stresses are faced each day by thousands of kids who do not kill themselves, but the suicidal young people are extremely anxious and see events as much more important than they really are. "This," he concludes, "is where therapy could play a big role in preventing suicide in the young."[10]

Finding Help

If you know someone who is a candidate for suicidal behavior, it is important to be aware of any stresses in the person's life that may pose an additional risk. Although it is not possible for parents to prevent problems that arise in their teenager's life, they need to be alert to obvious signs that might be an indication of suicidal behavior. If the teenager starts to give away prized possessions or make amends for past wrongdoings, for example, he or she may be thinking of suicide. When the teenager starts to actually talk about suicide, parents need to take immediate action.

First, parents and friends need to keep the lines of communication open. They may react to a teenager who has thoughts of suicide by denying the problem. "Oh, things are not that bad," they might say. This only makes the teenager feel like his or her feelings are not important, and that the parents or friends do not understand—so he or she stops confiding in them. Instead, parents and friends need to listen closely to what the teenager has to say. A person at risk of suicide needs to feel loved and secure, not judged. It must be clear that together you can work out the problems, and suicide

A depressed person needs help to regain the ability to live fully.

is not an acceptable choice.[11] There are also suicide hotlines and support groups all over the United States that are available to anyone feeling depressed or suicidal. To get the name of a crisis center or support group near you, write to the American Association of Suicidology, 2459 S. Ash, Denver, CO 80222.

The Problem of Stigmas

When talking to parents or calling a hotline is not enough to make the pain go away, a person who has thoughts of suicide should be evaluated by a mental health professional—a psychiatrist or psychologist. A good place to begin is often with a confidential discussion of the problem with a physician, guidance counselor, minister, or teacher. Someone who has the symptoms of major depression or manic-depressive illness should probably also be seen for evaluation by a mental health professional. But seeking outside help is not always easy. We often consider how society will react when we make this decision. Unfortunately, society often views depression as a sign of weakness. Therefore, many people do not get the help they need, because they are afraid that people will place a stigma on them as someone who is "mental" or has "emotional problems." Men have an especially difficult time admitting that they have problems. Instead of talking to someone, men may turn to alcohol or drugs as a way of dealing with their problems. Women are more likely to talk about their problems with another person. This may be one reason why statistics show that women are more likely to suffer from depression than men.

In addition to people's stereotyped reactions to those with mental illness, there are some troubling practical consequences of seeking aid for mood disorders. Applications for insurance policies routinely ask if you have been treated for mental disorders, and some companies may deny coverage if the answer is yes. People with a history of mental illness may also have trouble getting certain kinds of jobs if their medical records show treatment for mood disorders. Yet restricting the opportunities of people with affective disorders is unfair and probably also illegal, as specified by the Americans with Disabilities Act. At present there may not be a right answer to this dilemma. But as the concept of mental disorders as diseases becomes more widely accepted, and better means of diagnosing and curing such disorders are developed, the lingering stigmas should gradually disappear.

Although the problem of stigmas in society may be a grim reality, most people who do seek treatment for affective disorders would agree that the benefits can be immeasurable. As stated earlier, 80 percent of depressed patients respond positively to treatment and are able to enjoy fulfilling lives again.

8

Depression and the Future

In 1995 several books came out that claimed that the hormone melatonin stimulates the body's immune defenses against disease and can stop or even reverse some of the effects of aging. The books rapidly became best-sellers, and people flocked to health food stores to buy melatonin pills. Whether these claims are accurate or not, only time will tell. But it seems likely that this hormone may be an answer to the problems of some people with seasonal affective disorder (SAD).

Melatonin is the hormone that is released in the body only at night and that regulates the body's internal clock. The melatonin in SAD patients does not function properly, making their clock act as if it were a few hours earlier than the actual time. Scientists believe that a dose of melatonin can help to "reset" the biological clocks of SAD patients. Studies have shown that melatonin helps people with jet lag and people who work at jobs where they continually change shifts. Melatonin has actually cut down the amount of time it takes the body to adjust to a change in schedule. However, Dr. Alfred Lewy from the Oregon Health Sciences University in Portland, an expert on circadian rhythms (the daily variations of body functions), says that only tiny amounts of melatonin, much less than a milligram, are required to reset the body clock. But the melatonin that is sold over-the-counter comes in doses of two milligrams to even tens of milligrams. Such large doses will reset the body clock but will also cause sleepiness. This could cause a problem for someone who has jet lag or needs to start a night shift. It can also be dangerous for someone who needs to drive. Therefore, all products on the market recommend that melatonin should be taken shortly before going to sleep.[1]

Scientists are still struggling to find some definite answers about depressive illnesses that will bring about better diagnostic methods, better treatments, and possibly a way to prevent the disease from developing.

The Amish Study

In the 1980s, Dr. Janice Egeland, of the University of Miami School of Medicine, was conducting a study on the Old Order Amish in Lancaster County, Pennsylvania, in search of that "guilty gene" responsible for making some people susceptible to manic depression. The Amish seem like the perfect experimental group. They live their lives in much the same

Three visitors look at life-sized plaster statues of a depressed man, young woman, and teenage boy, from the Depression Awareness, Recognition, and Treatment Program.

way as they did when they came to America in the eighteenth century. Their community is stable and consists of large families. Everyone has roughly the same level of education. Since all members of the Amish community hold the same religious and moral traditions, they have almost no crime, violence, drug or alcohol abuse, or divorce. There are few, if any, outside influences that could make the results of the study biased. They seem basically pure. However, the Amish experience manic-depressive illness at the same rate as other communities.

In 1983 Dr. Egeland began spending time with the Amish, interviewing them and taking blood samples. In 1987, Dr. Egeland and her colleagues found what they were looking for after analyzing the DNA from the blood samples. They noticed almost 80 percent of the people who had a mutation (a genetic change) near the tip of the eleventh chromosome also had manic-depressive illness. This seemed to be a major breakthrough in understanding the origin of manic-depressive illness. In fact, the mutation appeared to be located near a gene that had already been identified and was known to be involved in the production of neurotransmitters.

The Amish study was then repeated by a team from the National Institute of Mental Health, which supported Dr. Egeland's findings. However, in 1989, new evidence cast doubts on the eleventh-chromosome link. The Amish study was then expanded to more family members and the researchers noticed that the earlier findings might have led to inaccurate conclusions. Two people from the original study who showed no signs of manic-depressive illness and had no defect on chromosome eleven later developed depressive disorders. This finding did not agree with the theory that the "depression gene" is on chromosome eleven.

Dr. Egeland is not totally convinced that her findings are wrong. One of the new findings involved a man who became depressed after his father had died. Depression would be a completely understandable reaction to that kind of stress, having nothing to do with genetics. The other person who later developed clinical depression was harder to explain in the light of Dr. Egeland's theory, however. Although he had no defect on chromosome eleven, he came from a family with a number of cases of manic-depressive illness. His many younger brothers and sisters did not show any signs of the illness, though they might develop it later.

The Amish study still continues, but some scientists now think that maybe there is more than one "guilty gene," or maybe it is in a different location. In a 1989 report, published in the scientific journal *Nature,* researchers reexamined the original Amish study and gave convincing evidence that the gene originally indicated in the study may not be involved at all. Meanwhile, other studies on different population groups have found indications of a link of depressive disorders with genes on other chromosomes.

At present, there are theories but no real answers. However, Dr. Egeland and other researchers are convinced that finding the gene or genes that are responsible for inheriting a tendency for manic-depressive illness is the key to developing good diagnostic tests and eventually a cure for this debilitating disease.[2]

In 1991, Dr. Egeland and three dozen prestigious researchers met in New York to discuss gene research for manic-depressive illness and schizophrenia. They decided that everyone should combine all of their research findings and compare notes, instead of drawing individual conclusions. If several people are working on the same problem, this could significantly speed up the process of finding the genetic link for these mental illnesses.[3]

A "Set Point" for Happiness?

Several studies reported in 1996 provide further support for the idea that a person's mood is determined to a large degree by heredity. Drs. David Lykken and Auke Tellegen, behavioral geneticists at the University of Minnesota, studied fifteen hundred pairs of twins, who rated their sense of well-being by answering true or false to statements such as "I am just naturally cheerful" and "The future looks bright to me." Identical twins, who have identical sets of genes, each rated their level of well-being about the same. This was the case even for pairs of identical twins who had been separated shortly after birth and raised by different families under quite different circumstances. Fraternal twins, who share about half of their genes (just like any two children of the same parents), had happiness scores only a little closer than those of unrelated pairs of people. Life circumstances, such as a person's salary, education, or marital status, determined very little of the differences between twins—and those who had more money, prestige, or education were no happier than their seemingly less well-off twin.

In another recent report, researchers at the National Institute on Aging analyzed the data of several studies that followed nearly six thousand people over a period of ten years. Although the well-being of each person varied from day to day, his or her typical mood was basically the same at the beginning and at the end of the study. Even major life traumas, like divorce or the death of a husband or wife, had only a temporary effect on a person's basic mood, which gradually faded over a year or so. Studies such as these prompted Dr. Edward Diener and his wife, Dr. Carol Diener, psychologists at the University of Illinois at Urbana, to propose that each person has a "set point" of happiness—a basic level to which his or her mood tends to return after fluctuations due to the good and bad experiences in life. This idea is similar to the set point theory of weight control, according to which the brain seems to turn the body's metabolism up or down depending on circumstances, to maintain the same basic weight. Some people seem to be naturally cheerful and optimistic, while others tend to look at the down side of things. Dr. Tellegen, a coauthor of the twin study, says that each person has not only a characteristic mood level but also a typical range of ups and downs; one person's mood may vary only a little, while another person may be "an emotional Pavarotti, with extreme ups and downs," but in each case the moods will average out and tend to return to the same basic level.[4]

SALLY FORTH

Dr. Richard Davidson, a psychologist at the University of Wisconsin, has found some patterns of brain activity that seem to be linked with a person's basic mood level. People for whom a PET scan of the brain shows a higher level of activity in the left front region tend to be more emotionally positive, energetic, and enthusiastic. People who are clinically depressed, on the contrary, show more activity in the right front region of the brain. These differences in brain activity patterns seem to be associated with the receptors for the neurotransmitter dopamine. Some pathways in the left front region of the brain, controlled by this neurochemical, are involved in positive emotions, and others inhibit signals of emotional distress. High dopamine levels in the brain have been linked with positive feelings. In January 1996, an Israeli research team found hereditary differences in the amount of dopamine the brain receptors bind, and these differences were related to the moods people experienced. Dr. Davidson notes, "it's the first time there's been a specific connection between a molecular genetic finding and people's levels of happiness."[5]

Researchers thus are gradually unraveling the complex mood-determining processes in the brain's molecular biology and tracing the role played by heredity. However, heredity is not the whole answer to solving the problem of depression and manic depression. These illnesses also seem to be triggered by environmental influences like stress. In some milder forms of the disorder, experience, rather than genetics, seems to play a major role. For instance, studies have shown that children of a depressed parent have a greatly increased risk of developing depression in later life. Environment could account for much of the increase. Depressed parents may raise their children in an inconsistent and irritable manner, making the child develop feelings of guilt and despair, which may lead to depression and other emotional problems.[6] The husband or wife of a depressed person is also at high risk of becoming clinically depressed. Psychologist Laura Rosen, of Columbia University, says that "depression can be contagious." She has found that people living with someone who is depressed have four times the usual risk of being depressed themselves and points out that couples therapy can be highly effective in preventing a relapse.[7]

A 1996 report by researchers in Berlin suggests that in some cases depression may be *literally* contagious. The Borna disease virus, which normally infects animals, was found in two patients with manic depression and one with major depression and chronic fatigue syndrome. In horses the virus causes episodes of listlessness and sleepiness; infected cats act depressed. Dr. Liv Bode, the author of the report, says that the virus might bring on an episode of depression in genetically susceptible people.[8]

Better Than Well?

Dr. Peter D. Kramer, a psychiatrist who has used drug therapy for depression extensively in his practice, reports that Prozac not only brought many of his patients out of deep depression but produced profound personality changes in some cases. Patients who were shy and inhibited before the treatment were transformed into confident, outgoing people under the influence of the drug. Some patients reported that they were able to think faster and work more effectively. Their family and friends were rather puzzled and disturbed at the dramatic changes in the people they had thought they knew. But the patients wanted to continue taking the drug; they did not want to lose the new, positive personalities they had gained. The drug had given them a new definition of feeling normal. It had not only made them well but had made them feel "better than well."[9]

Dr. Kramer felt uneasy with the idea of continuing to prescribe a drug for people who were no longer sick. But, could shyness and other personality traits be regarded as a sort of "subclinical illness" that kept people from functioning at their full potential? Would it be right to withhold a drug that had so few side effects from these patients? This is a question that seems destined to crop up more and more, he points out, as new, better mood-altering drugs are devised.[10]

Meanwhile, the wealth of new information researchers are gaining about the causes of depression and how it affects the body and mind is bringing a flood of new treatments to help bring people out of the depths of clinical depression. To some researchers, such as Dr. David Lykken, the growing knowledge about moods suggests a kind of recipe for living:

> A steady diet of simple pleasures will keep you above your set point. Find the small things that you know give you a little high—a good meal, working in the garden, time with friends—and sprinkle your life with them. In the long run, that will leave you happier than some grand achievement that gives you a big lift for a while.[11]

Q & A

Q. None of the things I used to enjoy doing seem like fun anymore, and when my friends ask me to go bowling or bike riding, I feel too tired to bother. Do I need vitamins or something?

A. Perhaps, but you may be suffering from depression. Take a look at the list of symptoms on p. 34–35 and see if there are any other items you recognize. If you have five or more symptoms, you should go to a doctor or a mental health clinic.

Q. My dog died last week, and I feel sad. I miss him and keep thinking about him. Do I need Prozac or something to feel better?

A. It is natural to feel sad after losing a loved one—and people can love pets very deeply—but gradually you should begin to feel better more of the time. If you still feel depressed after a few weeks, and find that your feelings are interfering with your life, it would be a good idea to see a doctor. A major stress could trigger depression in someone with a tendency for it.

Q. Is depression catching? A friend of mine is really down, and I feel pretty blue myself after I have been with her for a while.

A. There is no "depression germ" that you can catch, but it can take a lot of patience to stick by someone suffering from depression. Try to do plenty of things you enjoy during the time you are not with her.

Q. I'm worried about my boyfriend. Last winter he got real moody and kept saying life stinks and he's a failure and he might as well drop out of school or kill himself. Then he got over it and was a lot of fun again, but now it's like he's on speed or something—he talks so fast sometimes I can hardly understand him, and he's got these big plans, how he's going to play pro baseball and go to med school in the off season and make a million dollars in the stock market, but meanwhile he just lost his part-time job because he cursed out his boss. I asked him if he's on drugs, but he swears he isn't. Is he lying?

A. It sounds like he might have bipolar disorder. That extreme mood swing from depression to a reckless high sounds typical. You might try talking to his family or friends to see if they have noticed the same things you have. Perhaps someone can persuade him to get checked out by a doctor or mental health specialist. It might be difficult to persuade him now—people in a manic phase usually think they are just fine—but after he comes down and realizes what a mess he has been making of his life, he may be more willing to seek help.

Q. I've been kind of depressed, and my doctor prescribed an antidepressant. But I've been taking it for more than a week now, and I don't feel any better. My eyes seem blurry when I try to read, and I think the medicine is making me confused. What should I do?

A. Discuss the situation with your doctor. A week or two is not really enough time to tell whether the medication will help you or not, and it may be your depression rather than the drug that is making you confused. However, if the side effects are bothering you, the doctor may be able to substitute a different medication that will help you more effectively.

Q. I feel so down all the time lately. My parents got divorced, and I'm sure it was my fault because I used to hear them arguing about me. And I'm not even worth it—I'm not good at sports, and I'm flunking math, and I don't have any friends in this new town we moved to after the divorce. Now my mom says she wants to take me to a psychiatrist, but I don't want people to think I'm crazy!

A. You are not crazy, but you do sound rather depressed. That happens to lots of people, and getting help for it is nothing to be ashamed of. Depression is an illness. Nothing you did caused it. But there are treatments available now to help nearly everyone who suffers from depression, so you do not have to keep feeling so bad.

Q. My friend says she is feeling really depressed, and sometimes she even thinks about killing herself. But she made me promise not to tell her parents or anybody. Would I be a snitch if I told our counselor at school?

A. Normally you should keep promises, but in a situation like this, your friend could be in real danger. The sooner she gets help, the better. It would be a good idea to discuss the problem with your counselor or some other sympathetic adult who can make some tactful suggestions to your friend and her family.

Q. My doctor says I'm bipolar and put me on lithium. It really worked and I'm feeling fine now, but she says I have to keep taking the drug. I don't like the idea of being on drugs.

A. People with bipolar disorder have a problem with their brain biochemistry, and lithium helps to keep the brain chemicals in the proper balance. Just as people with diabetes have to keep taking insulin all their lives, you need to continue taking lithium to keep from going into another manic-depressive cycle.

Depression Timeline

400 B.C.—Hippocrates described melancholia (depression); Democritus studied the causes and treatments of melancholia.

A.D. 100s—Soranus treated depression and manic depression with mineral water.

1514—Albrecht Dürer completed the engraving *Melancholia I.*

1621—Robert Burton published *The Anatomy of Melancholy.*

mid-1800s—Jean Etienne Esquirol noted the seasonal nature of some depressions.

1890s—Sigmund Freud first presented his ideas on psychoanalysis.

early 1900s—Emil Kraepelin described manic depression.

1948—Mary Jane Ward's novel *The Snake Pit* was published and made into a hit movie dealing with shock therapy treatment for mental illness.

1949—John Cade discovered lithium's effects on manic patients.

1950s—The anti-tuberculosis drug iproniazid was found to have antidepressive action.

1951—Patent issued for imipramine, the first tricyclic antidepressant.

1960s—Monoamine oxidase inhibitors were first used as antidepressants.

1970—The FDA approved lithium as a treatment for manic depression.

1974—Fluoxetine (Prozac) was found to inhibit reabsorption of serotonin by nerve cells.

1984—Norman E. Rosenthal identified seasonal affective disorder (SAD) and suggested light therapy.

1987—American Psychiatric Association recognized SAD as a mental disorder.

For More Information

Information and help for various forms of depression can be obtained from local physicians and mental health specialists, community mental health centers, psychiatric clinics, universities or medical schools, and family service agencies. The following sources offer helpful pamphlets and information about referrals and support groups:

American Psychiatric Association
1400 K Street, N.W.
Suite 1101
Washington, DC 20005
(800) 368-5777

DEPRESSION Awareness, Recognition, and Treatment (D/ART), NIMH
5600 Fishers Lane, Room 10-85
Rockville, MD 20857
(301) 443-4140; (800) 421-4211
NIMH publications by fax: (301) 443-5158

Lithium Information Center
Dean Foundation
8000 Excelsior Drive, Suite 208
Madison, WI 53717
(608) 836-8070

National Alliance for the Mentally Ill
2101 Wilson Boulevard, Suite 302
Arlington, VA 22201
(703) 524-7600; (800) 950-NAMI[6264]

National Depressive and Manic Depressive Association (NDMDA)
730 N. Franklin, Suite 501
Chicago, IL 60610
(312) 642-0049; (800) 826-3632
(800) 82-NDMDA

National Foundation for Depressive Illness
P.O. Box 2257
New York, NY 10116
(800) 248-4344

National Mental Health Association
1021 Prince Street
Alexandria, VA 22314
(703) 684-7722; (800) 969-NMHA

Chapter Notes

Chapter 1

1. Paul M. Angle, "Lincoln, Abraham," *The World Book Encyclopedia* (Chicago: World Book, Inc., 1988), vol. 12, p. 315; David B. Cohen, *Out of the Blue: Depression and Human Nature* (New York: Norton, 1994), p. 45; Richard Nelson Current, "Lincoln, Abraham," *Encyclopaedia Britannica* (Chicago: Encyclopaedia Britannica, 1973), vol. 14, p. 46; J. Raymond DePaulo, Jr., and Keith Russell Ablow, *How to Cope with Depression* (New York: McGraw-Hill, 1989), p. 31.

2. Cohen, p. 45.

3. Ibid.

Chapter 2

1. I Samuel 16:1–31:13 Samuel 1:1–5:3 *The Bible.*

2. Francis Mark Mondimore, *Depression: The Mood Disease* (Baltimore: Johns Hopkins University Press, 1990), p. 5.

3. E. Cobham Brewer, *Brewer's Dictionary of Phrase and Fable,* 11th ed., revised by John Freeman (New York: Harper & Row, 1968), p. 473.

4. *New International Illustrated Encyclopedia of Art* (New York: Greystone Press, 1967–71), vol. 7, p. 1411.

5. "On the Subject of . . . Depression: From Moods to Melancholia," *The Pennsylvania Gazette,* December 1990, p. 36.

6. *Encyclopaedia Britannica* (Chicago: Encyclopaedia Britannica, 1973), vol. 4, pp. 462–463.

7. David B. Cohen, *Out of the Blue: Depression and Human Nature* (New York: Norton, 1994), p. 80.

8. J. Raymond DePaulo, Jr., and Keith Russell Ablow, *How to Cope with Depression* (New York: McGraw-Hill, 1989), p. 61.

9. Robert N. Moreines and Patricia L. McGuire, *Light Up Your Blues: Understanding and Overcoming Seasonal Affective Disorders* (Washington, D.C.: The PIA Press, 1989), p. 13.

10. "Light can help you from getting SAD," *The Courier-News* (Bridgewater, N.J.), December 6, 1994, p. B6.

11. DePaulo, Jr., and Ablow, p. 51.

12. Mondimore, p. 62.

13. Demitri Papolos and Janice Papolos, *Overcoming Depression* (New York: Harper & Row, 1987), p. 87.

14. Ben Fischman, "The Case for Shock Treatment," *Psychology Today,* September 1989, p. 75.

15. Richard Abrams, "Out of the Blue," *The Sciences,* November/December 1989, p. 25.

16. Barbara D. Ingersoll and Sam Goldstein, *Lonely, Sad and Angry: A Parent's Guide to Depression in Children and Adolescents* (New York: Doubleday, 1995), p. 106.

17. Papolos and Papolos, p. 89.

18. Patty Duke and Gloria Hochman, *A Brilliant Madness: Living with Manic-Depressive Illness* (New York: Bantam, 1992), p. 119.

19. Papolos and Papolos, p. 87.

20. Duke and Hochman, p. 124.

21. Ingersoll and Goldstein, pp. 76–77, 98.

Chapter 3

1. Mary Maushard, "Mike Wallace tells of battle with depression," *The Courier-News* (Bridgewater, N.J.), April 20, 1991, p. B3.

2. Kathy Cronkite, *On the Edge of Darkness: Conversations about Conquering Depression* (New York: Doubleday, 1994), p. 14; Erica E. Goode with Nancy Linnon and Sarah Burke, "Beating Depression," *U.S. News & World Report,* March 5, 1990, p. 50.

3. Cronkite, pp. 14–15.

4. Patty Duke and Gloria Hochman, *A Brilliant Madness: Living with Manic-Depressive Illness* (New York: Bantam, 1992), p. 1.

5. "Patty Duke talks about her battle with illness," *The Courier-News* (Bridgewater, N.J.), October 6, 1989, p. B12.

6. Ibid.; Goode, p. 51; Tim Warren, "Stars change attitudes on manic depression," *The Courier-News* (Bridgewater, N.J.), July 2, 1992, p. B7.

7. Merriam-Webster's Collegiate Dictionary, 10th ed. (Springfield, Mass.: Merriam-Webster, 1993).

8. National Institute of Mental Health, *Depression: What Every Woman Should Know,* NIH Publication No. 95-3871 (Rockville, Md.: DEPRESSION Awareness, Recognition, and Treatment (D/ART) Campaign, 1995), p. 1; National Institute of Mental Health, *Plain Talk About . . . Depression,* NIH Publication No. 94-3561 (Rockville, Md.: National Institutes of Health, 1994).

9. National Institute of Mental Health, *Depression: What Every Woman Should Know,* NIH Publication No. 95-3871, p. 2.

10. Jane E. Brody, "Personal Health: Depression in the Elderly: Old Notions Hinder Help," *The New York Times,* February 9, 1994, p. C13.

11. Simeon Margolis and Peter V. Rabins, *Depression and Anxiety* (Baltimore, Md.: Johns Hopkins Medical Institutions, 1994), p. 5.

12. Barbara D. Ingersoll and Sam Goldstein, *Lonely, Sad and Angry: A Parent's Guide to Depression in Children and Adolescents* (New York: Doubleday, 1995), pp. 4–9.

13. Peter D. Kramer, *Listening to Prozac: A Psychiatrist Explores Antidepressant Drugs and the Remaking of the Self* (New York: Viking Penguin, 1993), pp. 115–122.

14. National Institute of Mental Health, *Depression: What Every Woman Should Know,* p. 5.

15. Margolis and Rabins, p. 6; Donald F. Klein and Paul H. Wender, *Understanding Depression: A Complete Guide to Its Diagnosis and Treatment* (New York: Oxford University Press, 1993), p. 90.

16. Kramer, pp. 131–135.

17. J. Raymond DePaulo, Jr., and Keith Russell Ablow, *How to Cope with Depression* (New York: McGraw-Hill, 1989), p. 78.

18. National Institute of Mental Health, *Bipolar Disorder,* NIH Publication No. 93-3679 (Rockville, Md.: National Institutes of Health, 1993), pp. 4–5.

19. Arthur Hirsch, "Red-Hot and Blue," *The Star-Ledger* (Newark, N.J.), August 1, 1995, Section 6, p. 1.

20. Jane E. Brody, "Personal Health: Debate Aside, Melatonin Can Reset the Body's Clock," *The New York Times,* September 27, 1995, p. C9.

Chapter 4

1. Joseph Alper, "Depression at an Early Age: It Strikes in Childhood, and It's on the Rise," *Science 86,* May 1986, p. 45.

2. Ibid., pp. 45–46.

3. Ibid., p. 46.

4. Barbara D. Ingersoll and Sam Goldstein, *Lonely, Sad and Angry: A Parent's Guide to Depression in Children and Adolescents* (New York: Doubleday, 1995), pp. 41–42.

5. Ibid., p. 48.

6. Jane E. Brody, "Personal Health: Depression in the Elderly: Old Notions Hinder Help," *The New York Times,* February 9, 1994, p. C13.

7. Ingersoll and Goldstein, p. 49.

8. Ibid., p. 46.

9. J. Raymond DePaulo, Jr., and Keith Russell Ablow, *How to Cope with Depression* (New York: McGraw-Hill, 1989), p. 131.

Chapter 5

1. "Out of the darkness: One girl's diary of depression," *'Teen,* April 1995, pp. 52–54.

2. National Institute of Mental Health, *Depression—Effective Treatments are Available,* NIH Publication No. 3590 (Rockville, Md.: Public Health Service, 1994), p. 93.

3. "Imipramine Hydrochloride," *Physicians' GenRx* (St. Louis: Mosby Yearbook, Inc., 1996), p. II–1129.

4. Peter D. Kramer, *Listening to Prozac* (New York: Viking Penguin, 1993), pp. 55, 57.

5. Ibid., p. 63.

6. Associated Press, "Chemical Linked to Binge Eating," *The New York Times,* May 28, 1993, p. A18.

7. Sally Hamilton, "Why the Lady Loves $C_6H_5(CH_2)2NH_2$," *New Scientist,* December 19/26, 1992, p. 26.

8. Simeon Margolis and Peter V. Rabins, *Depression and Anxiety* (Baltimore, Md.: Johns Hopkins Medical Institutions, 1994), pp. 14, 17.

9. Barbara D. Ingersoll and Sam Goldstein, *Lonely, Sad and Angry: A Parent's Guide to Depression in Children and Adolescents* (New York: Doubleday, 1995), pp. 100–108.

10. Ibid., pp. 78–93.

11. Ibid., pp. 120–121; Norman E. Rosenthal, *Winter Blues* (New York: Guilford Press, 1993), pp. 99–123.

12. Ingersoll and Goldstein, pp. 119–120; Richard Abrams, "Out of the Blue," *The Sciences,* November-December 1989, pp. 25–30.

13. Dick Cavett, "Goodbye, Darkness," *People,* August 3, 1992, pp. 88–90.

14. Ingersoll and Goldstein, pp. 133–138.

Chapter 6

1. Jane E. Brody, "Personal Health: Boning Up on Possible Mental and Physical Health Needs of Children Who Are Bound for College," *The New York Times,* August 24, 1989, p. B12.

2. "40 Ways to Beat Stress," *Home Library Special Report,* November-December 1992, pp. 3–14.

Chapter 7

1. Editors of Time-Life Books, *Emotions, Journey Through the Mind and Body Series* (Alexandria, Va.: Time-Life Books, 1994), p. 118.

2. Patty Duke and Gloria Hochman, *A Brilliant Madness: Living with Manic-Depressive Illness* (New York: Bantam, 1992), p. 182.

3. Ibid., pp. 182–183; Erica E. Goode with Nancy Linnon and Sarah Burke, "Beating Depression," *U.S. News and World Report,* March 5, 1990, p. 51.

4. Duke and Hochman, pp. 184–185.

5. Ibid., pp. 50–51.

6. Barbara D. Ingersoll and Sam Goldstein, *Lonely, Sad and Angry: A Parent's Guide to Depression in Children and Adolescents* (New York: Doubleday, 1995), pp. 122, 124; Jane E. Brody, "Suicide Myths Cloud Efforts to Save Children," *The New York Times,* June 16, 1992, p. C1.

7. National Institute of Mental Health, *Suicide Facts,* NIH Publication No. 94-4081, (Rockville, Md.: National Institutes of Health, 1996); Barbara D. Ingersoll and Sam Goldstein, pp. 124–127.

8. D. A. Nielsen, D. Goldman, et al., "Suicidality and 5-hydroxyincoleacetic acid concentration associated with a tryptophan hydroxylase polymorphism," *Archives of General Psychiatry,* vol. 51, 1994, pp. 34–38.

9. Brody, p. C3.

10. Ibid.

11. Ingersoll and Goldstein, pp. 131–133.

Chapter 8

1. Jane E. Brody, "Experimental Evidence Is Lacking for Melatonin as Cure-All: Optimism Exceeds Test Results in Humans" and "Personal Health: Debate Aside, Melatonin Can Reset the Body's Clock," *The New York Times,* September 27, 1995, p. C9.

2. Patty Duke and Gloria Hochman, *A Brilliant Madness: Living with Manic-Depressive Illness* (New York: Bantam, 1992), pp. 72–77; Erica E. Goode with Nancy Linnon and Sarah Burke, "Beating Depression," *U.S. News and World Report,* March 5, 1990, p. 55.

3. Duke and Hochman, pp. 78–79.

4. Daniel Goleman, "Forget Money; Nothing Can Buy Happiness, Some Researchers Say," *The New York Times,* July 16, 1996, p. C9.

5. Ibid.

6. Demitri Papolos and Janice Papolos, *Overcoming Depression* (New York: Harper & Row, 1987), pp. 120–121.

7. Myron B. Pitts, "'Contagious' Depression," *USA Weekend,* October 11–13, 1996, p. 12.

8. Associated Press, "Virus May Be Linked to Depression," *The New York Times,* July 23, 1996, p. C10.

9. Peter D. Kramer, *Listening to Prozac* (New York: Viking, 1993), pp. x–xi.

10. Ibid., pp. 1–21.

11. Goleman, p. C9.

Glossary

affective disorder—An illness that involves a disturbance of feelings or emotions.

antidepressant drug—Medication to relieve clinical depression.

ATP—A chemical the body uses to store energy.

axon—A single long, thin strand extending from a nerve cell that transmits outgoing signals to other nerve cells.

behavioral therapy—A type of psychotherapy that treats depression as learned behavior that must be "unlearned."

bipolar disorder—Manic-depressive illness.

borderline personality disorder—A psychiatric condition that involves unstable relationships with others, extreme mood changes, and difficulties in controlling intense anger.

circadian rhythms—Cyclic variations of various body functions, timed to the twenty-four-hour day.

clinical depression—Depression that is long lasting and/or impairs a person's ability to function normally.

cognitive therapy—A type of psychotherapy that is based on the idea that people who think negatively about themselves, the world, and the future will develop feelings of depression and despair. Patients are trained to replace negative thought patterns with positive ones.

cortisol—A hormone secreted by the adrenal gland when a person is under stress.

dendrites—Thin branches of nerve cells that receive incoming signals.

dexamethasone suppression test (DST)—A diagnostic test that can indicate depression by showing increased levels of cortisol.

dopamine—A type of neurotransmitter that helps to regulate mood.

dysthymia—A mild form of depression that is chronic and long term, lasting for months or even years at a time.

electroconvulsive therapy (ECT)—Also known as shock therapy; a type of treatment that produces convulsions (seizures) in severely depressed patients to improve their mood.

euphoria—A "high;" a mood of extreme happiness and elation.

family therapy—A type of psychotherapy that requires the entire family to participate in a therapy session and talk out their problems together.

fluoxetine—Prozac (an antidepressant drug).

insight-oriented therapy—A type of psychotherapy that digs into the subconscious and gains insight into the person's painful experiences.

interpersonal psychotherapy—A type of psychological treatment that is based on the idea that people become depressed because of problems that arise within relationships with family or friends.

light therapy—A method of treatment for SAD patients in which "light boxes" are used to provide enough light to relieve their depression.

lithium—The most commonly prescribed medication for manic-depressive patients.

magnetic resonance imaging (MRI)—A diagnostic test that provides pictures of the inner structures of the brain by detecting signals emitted by the nuclei of different types of atoms in a magnetic field.

major depression—Also known as unipolar depression; the most severe form of depression—patients have little or no control over their lives, making it difficult to function normally in everyday activities.

manic-depressive illness—Also known as bipolar disorder; a form of depression that involves cycles of extreme happiness and utter despair.

melancholia—An ancient word used to describe depression.

melatonin—A hormone released into the bloodstream by the pineal gland only at night. It regulates a person's internal body clock, helping to adjust to the changing environmental conditions of day and night.

monoamine oxidase—An enzyme in the nervous system that breaks down neurotransmitters.

monoamine oxidase inhibitors (MAOIs)—A group of antidepressant drugs, such as isocarboxazid (Marplan) and phenelzine (Nardil), usually prescribed only to severely depressed patients.

neurons—Nerve cells.

neurotransmitters—Special chemicals released by neurons that carry the message across the synapse and spark the next neuron to fire in turn.

norepinephrine—A type of neurotransmitter that helps to regulate mood.

pituitary gland—A small structure deep inside the brain that secretes the body's hormones.

positron emission tomography (PET)—A diagnostic test that uses medical imaging to monitor brain functioning.

postsynaptic neurons—The neurons to which the nerve impulses are transmitted.

psychotherapy—Various forms of psychological treatment that involve talking with a therapist to understand and resolve conflicts.

receptors—Special chemicals on the surface of the neurons that receive neurotransmitters.

reuptake—Reabsorption of a neurotransmitter by the neuron that released it.

seasonal affective disorder (SAD)—A form of depression that occurs usually during the fall and winter months when there is decreased sunlight.

selective serotonin reuptake inhibitors (SSRIs)—A group of antidepressant drugs that include fluoxetine (Prozac).

serotonin—A type of neurotransmitter that helps to regulate mood.

sleep electroencephalogram (EEG)—A diagnostic test that measures brain electrical activity during sleep.

synapse—A tiny, fluid-filled gap between nerve cells, through which messages are carried by neurotransmitters.

thematic apperception test—A personality test that involves interpreting pictures. This gives insight into a person's needs, fears, and struggles.

tricyclic antidepressants—A group of antidepressant drugs, such as imipramine (Tofranil) and desipramine (Norpramin), named for their chemical structure, which includes three rings of carbon atoms.

whole-body illness—A disease that affects every aspect of a person's life—physical, emotional, and social.

Further Reading

Books

Cohen, David B. *Out of the Blue: Depression and Human Nature.* New York: Norton, 1994.

Cronkite, Kathy. *On the Edge of Darkness: Conversations about Conquering Depression.* New York: Doubleday, 1994.

DePaulo, J. Raymond, Jr., and Keith Russell Ablow. *How to Cope with Depression.* New York: McGraw-Hill, 1989.

Duke, Patty and Gloria Hochman. *A Brilliant Madness: Living with Manic-Depressive Illness.* New York: Bantam, 1992.

Ingersoll, Barbara D. and Sam Goldstein. *Lonely, Sad and Angry: A Parent's Guide to Depression in Children and Adolescents.* New York: Doubleday, 1995.

Klein, Donald F. and Paul H. Wender. *Understanding Depression: A Complete Guide to Its Diagnosis and Treatment.* New York: Oxford University Press, 1993.

Kramer, Peter D. *Listening to Prozac: A Psychiatrist Explores Antidepressant Drugs and the Remaking of the Self.* New York: Viking Penguin, 1993.

Margolis, Simeon and Peter V. Rabins. *Depression and Anxiety.* The Johns Hopkins White Papers. Baltimore: The Johns Hopkins Medical Institutions, 1994.

Mondimore, Francis Mark. *Depression: The Mood Disease.* Baltimore: The Johns Hopkins University Press, 1990.

Moreines, Robert N. and Patricia McGuire. *Light Up Your Blues.* Washington, D.C.: The PIA Press, 1989.

Papolos, Demitri F. and Janice Papolos. *Overcoming Depression.* New York: Harper & Row, 1987.

Preston, John. *You Can Beat Depression.* San Luis Obispo, Calif.: Impact, 1989, 1996.

Rosenthal, Norman E. *Winter Blues: Seasonal Affective Disorder: What It Is and How to Overcome It.* New York: Guilford Press, 1993.

Pamphlets

American Psychiatric Association:

Depression
Manic-Depressive/Bipolar Disorder
Teen Suicide

DEPRESSION Awareness, Recognition, and Treatment (D/ART) Campaign:

Depression: What Every Woman Should Know
D/ART Fact Sheet

National Institute of Mental Health:

Bipolar Disorder
Depressive Illnesses: Treatments Bring New Hope
Helpful Facts about Depressive Illnesses
Lithium

Public Health Service:

Depression: Effective Treatments Are Available
Depression: What You Need to Know
Helping the Depressed Person Get Treatment

Articles

Abrams, Richard. "Out of the Blue: The Rehabilitation of Electroconvulsive Therapy." *The Sciences,* November-December 1989, pp. 25–30.

Alper, Joseph. "Depression at an Early Age: It Strikes in Childhood and It's on the Rise." *Science 86,* May 1986, pp. 45–50.

Angier, Natalie. "Scientists Now Say They Can't Find a Gene for Manic-Depressive Illness." *The New York Times,* January 13, 1993, p. C12.

Borne, Ronald F. "Serotonin: The Neurotransmitter for the '90s." *Drug Topics,* October 10, 1994, pp. 108–115.

Bower, Bruce. "Moods and the Muse." *Science News,* June 17, 1995, pp. 378–380.

———. "Truth Aches." *Science News,* August 15, 1992, pp. 110–111.

Brody, Jane E. "Suicide Myths Cloud Efforts to Save Children." *The New York Times,* June 16, 1992, pp. C1, C3.

Brower, Montgomery. "If Winter's Gloom Gives You the Blues, Norman Rosenthal May Be Able to Lighten Your Mood." *People,* January 11, 1988, pp. 115–116.

Cavett, Dick. "Goodbye, Darkness." *People,* August 3, 1992, pp. 88–90.

Chollar, Susan. "Beating Bad Moods." *American Health,* November 1992, pp. 55–58.

"Does Therapy Work?" *Consumer Reports,* November 1995, pp. 734–739.

Dowling, Colette. "Rescuing Your Child from Depression." *New York,* January 20, 1992, pp. 44–53.

Elmer-Dewitt, Philip. "Depression: The Growing Role of Drug Therapies." *Time,* July 6, 1992, pp. 56–60.

Freudenheim, Milt. "The Drug Makers Are Listening to Prozac." *The New York Times,* January 9, 1994, p. 7.

Goleman, Daniel. "The Brain Manages Happiness and Sadness in Different Centers." *The New York Times,* March 28, 1995, pp. C1, C9.

———. "Forget Money; Nothing Can Buy Happiness, Some Researchers Say." *The New York Times,* July 16, 1996, pp. C1, C9.

———. "New View of Prozac: It's Good But It's Not a Wonder Drug." *The New York Times,* October 19, 1994, p. C11.

———. "The Quiet Comeback of Electroshock Therapy." *Encyclopedia Science Supplement,* 1993, pp. 154–157.

———. "Why Girls Are Prone to Depression." *The New York Times,* May 10, 1990, p. B15.

———."Women's Depression Rate Is Higher." *The New York Times,* December 6, 1990, p. B18.

Goode, Erica E., with Nancy Linnon and Sarah Burke. "Beating Depression." *U.S. News & World Report,* March 5, 1990, pp. 48–56.

Griffin, Katherine. "The Unbearable Darkness of Being." *In Health,* January/February 1991, pp. 62–67.

Jamison, Kay Redfield. "Manic-Depressive Illness and Creativity." *Scientific American,* February 1995, pp. 62–67.

Konner, Melvin. "Art of Darkness." *The Sciences,* November-December 1989, pp. 2–3.

"Multiple Genes for Manic Depression." *New Scientist,* March 12, 1987, p. 23.

Schmeck, Harold M., Jr. "Scientists Now Doubt They Found Faulty Gene Linked to Mental Illness." *The New York Times,* November 7, 1989, p. C3.

Stone, Gene. "Short Sharp Shocks." *New York,* November 14, 1994, pp. 55–59.

Thomas, Patricia. "Depression: Younger Patients, Newer Therapies." *Medical World News,* August 1990, pp. 28–36.

Toufexis, Anastasia. "Dark Days, Darker Spirits." *Time,* January 11, 1988, p. 66.

Wallis, Claudia. "Is Mental Illness Inherited?" *Time,* March 9, 1987, p. 67.

Wartig, Nancy. "Defeating Depression." *American Health,* December 1993, pp. 38–45, 86.

Weintraub, Pamela. "Warning: Side Effects." *American Health,* April 1992, pp. 36–37.

Internet Resources

http://earth.execpc.com/~corbeau/best/html
(Taylor, Dennis. Depression Resources List.)

http://earth.execpc.com/~corbeau/asdfaq.txt alt.support.depression
FAQ (Frequently Asked Questions.)

http://earth.execpc.com/~corbeau/best.html
(Best Things to Say to Someone Who Is Depressed.)

http://greed.isca.uiowa.edu/users/david-caropreso/depression.html
(Hemann, Lynda, and David Caropreso. The Depression Home Page.)

http://members.aol.com/depress/whatis.htm
(What is Depression (and what it is not)?)

http://members.aol.com/depress/screen.htm
(Clinical Depression Self-Screening Test.)

http://www.geocities.com/HotSprings/1872/depression.html
(Depression: Links to Information.)

http://www.healthguide.com/MHealth/default.stm
    (Health Guide Mental Health (includes descriptions of depression and bipolar disorder, diagnosis, types of therapy, and case histories.)

http://www.medaccess.com/guides/cpgs/cpg_1f.htm
    (Depression Is a Treatable Illness: A Patient's Guide.)

http://www.mentalhealth.com/mag1/p5h-dp01.html
    (How Much Does Depression Cost Society? The Harvard Mental Health Letter, October 1994.)

http://www.nami.org/namihome.htm
    (National Alliance for the Mentally Ill.)

http://www.nimh.nih.gov/dart/index.htm
    (DEPRESSION Awareness, Recognition, and Treatment (D/ART) PROGRAM.)

http://www.psycom.net/depression.central.html
    (Dr. Ivan's Depression Central.)

http://www.save.org/question.html
    (Questions Most Frequently Asked on Suicide.)

http://www.geocities.com/HotSprings/2836/mood.html
    (Pleasant, Sarah. My Experience with a Mood Disorder by (personal experiences and many links to online information sources), © 1996.)

Index